"In this inspiring book, you v men and women on mission for Christ. You will read of personal sometimes difficult struggles, but you will be blessed by those who have been committed to the cause of missions without failing. Wanda's life has been one of absolute commitment to the call of missions upon her life and the encouragement of others to be involved in God's Great Commission task. As a personal friend of Wanda, I can assure you that her integrity and her character undergird the authenticity of this new book. I commend her in this new work to you without hesitation."

—Dr. Frank S. Page, president, Executive Committee of the Southern Baptist Convention, and author of *The Nehemiah Factor: 16 Characteristics of a Missional Leader*

"You'll be 'plowing new ground' in this collection of stories of faith, courage, and missional living written by my friend Wanda Lee. You will also be inspired as she reminds us in the words of author George Eliot, 'It is never too late to be what you might have been.' Read this great book demonstrating the power of a good story!"

—Dr. Gordon Fort, vice-president, Office of Global Strategy, International Mission Board

"Wanda Lee has the ability to connect with her readers by relating personal experiences in such a way that they become real. Her practicality clearly stands as one of her best-developed skills and this is seen in all she writes and says. Anyone searching for a heartfelt narration of how God can work in our lives needs to have this book!"

—Linda Clark, women's specialist, Graceland Baptist Church, New Albany, Indiana, and author of *5 Leadership Essentials for Women* and *Awaken the Leader in You*

"Wanda Lee masterfully tells her life story, intertwined with stories from Scripture, missionary stories, and other real-life stories of God's amazing love and grace. As she weaves these stories together, the reader comes to see that they are part of the Story, the Story that Jesus has for us all as His children. She challenges you to relook at your own story, your part of His wonderful Story of grace as you continue the next chapter of serving the Lord."

—Kaye Miller, former national WMU president

OTHER NEW HOPE BOOKS BY WANDA S. LEE

*The Story Lives On* (Spanish)*:*
*Sigue la historia: El poder de Dios en toda*
*generación*

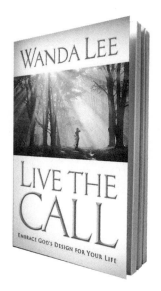

*Live the Call: Embrace God's*
*Design for Your Life*

*Live the Call* (Spanish)*:*
*Vive el llamado: Haga suyo el plan de Dios*
*para su vida*

# the Story Lives On

God's Power Throughout Generations

# WANDA S. LEE

## the Story Lives On

### God's Power Throughout Generations

**NEW HOPE**
PUBLISHERS

Birmingham, Alabama

New Hope® Publishers
P. O. Box 12065
Birmingham, AL 35202-2065
newhopedigital.com
New Hope Publishers is a division of WMU®.

Library of Congress Cataloging-in-Publication Data

Lee, Wanda, 1949-
  The story lives on : God's power throughout generations / Wanda S.
Lee.
    p. cm.
  ISBN 978-1-59669-344-9 (sc)
  1. Lee, Wanda, 1949- 2. Christian biography--United States. I.
Title.
  BR1725.L275A3 2012
  277.3'082092--dc23
  [B]
                        2012003272

ISBN-10: 1-59669-344-4
ISBN-13: 978-1-59669-344-9
N124149 • 0412 • 4M1

Cover design: Michel Lê
Interior design: Michel Lê

"We cannot help speaking about what we have seen and heard."                              —Acts 4:20

Contents

# Acknowledgments

*The story of faith is a* personal journey for each of us. Without the collective interaction with people who have crossed our paths, our stories would be rather bland. I have been blessed by a number of church families who were instrumental in the development of my faith story. From those in Florida who introduced me to Christ and nurtured me as a young believer, to Alabama where my church in high school and college helped me discover God's call in my life, I am most grateful. Who I have become as an adult is in large part due to the faithful teaching you provided for me and so many others during our youth.

As an adult I have been blessed by churches where my husband served as pastor and found great joy in being a part of many stories that made up our life as a church family. Gilgal Baptist Church in Tuscaloosa, Alabama, and Waldrop Memorial Baptist Church in Columbus, Georgia, allowed me to stretch and use my gifts in ways that helped me grow as a Christian. Without their encouragement and mentoring, my story would not include a call to missions and a love for the organization I lead today, WMU®.

To those who have allowed me to tell their story within the pages of this book, I am grateful for your faithfulness to Christ and His mission in the world. Your example of following Christ challenged me to examine my own life at various junctures and follow more closely. To the staff who helped these stories come alive on the printed page, thank you.

No other part of my story has been more fulfilling than the love of my family, a husband who makes it possible for me to lead WMU during this stage of my life, children who bring me joy and a sense of pride each day as I watch how they and their spouses live their faith, and especially my young grandsons who help keep me grounded in what is most important in life. Without each of you my story and my calling would not be nearly as rich and meaningful. And so the story lives on . . . stories of faith, joy, and hope because of the One we serve and who makes our stories possible. To Him be praise.

# Introduction

*S*itting on a small easel on my kitchen counter is a plaque given to me by my daughter. It says simply, "Home is where your story begins." *Home* has different meanings for different people. For some, home was a happy place with warm memories of family gatherings and positive experiences. For others, it means feelings of isolation, fear, even tears. What we share is the simple fact that it is the place where our personal stories begin.

My story, like yours, is a reflection of all the experiences that have made my life what it is today, but the foundation of that story was laid at home as a child. Those early impressions and values were gleaned as I experienced life at home. I've lived in many different places, each leaving a lasting imprint upon who I am.

*After I was born, my family moved from Alabama to Detroit, Michigan. I learned to say "school," "cool," and "you guys" with the accent of a Michigan native, much to the chagrin of my Southern grandparents. After three hard winters my father announced, "We're moving as far away from snow as possible," and we landed in Miami, Florida. The next ten years were spent in three different cities in south Florida where going to the beach and enjoying year-round summer was the norm.*

*Looking back, I realize we didn't stay in one place very long; but home is not about* where *as much as it is about* whom. *During those years, home was being with my parents and my brother.*

*My faith journey began early in life because my parents were Christian believers and exposed me to the teachings of the church almost from the day I was born. I was taught Scripture in Sunday School classes, at Vacation*

Bible School in the summertime, and through regular worship attendance. The year I turned 8 years old our church held what was commonly called spring revival services. One night my older brother made his way to the front of the church and professed his faith in Christ. Later in the week I followed and on Easter Sunday night we were baptized together by our pastor. I will never forget standing in the water with my brother sharing this important commitment. But this experience was just the beginning. What I knew in my head from my earliest days, that Jesus loved me and I loved Him, I now knew in my heart and I wanted to follow Him.

When I was 12, my mother was diagnosed with a malignant brain tumor. For two years we tried to keep life at home as normal as possible, but eventually decided she needed to be close to her family during her final months. My mom was one of 11 siblings, and with their help she was loved and cared for in a special way until the end. For me it meant I was able to stay in school. The downside was the two of us were forced to leave home and move back to Alabama, resulting in separation from my brother and dad, who remained in Florida.

And then, just prior to Christmas of my senior year in high school, she died. With all of the upheaval in my life during my teen years, the one constant was the presence of Christ, walking with me and guiding me in every decision.

On two different occasions, once in middle school and later in college, I recommitted my life to following Christ. My knowledge of His teachings was growing and my heart commitment followed. Both were significant decisions at critical turning points in my maturing as a young person and as a believer. The church was instrumental in my spiritual growth and understanding of what it meant to follow Christ during these years. Blessed by wonderful mentors and pastors, I was led to ask the hard questions about my future, the choices I would make regarding education and profession as well as marriage. Looking back, I realize it was foundational for the story that would eventually become *my own, the story of God's amazing love and grace that would carry me throughout my life.*

*While the rest of my story has many twists and turns, there has been one constant. From early on I felt a deep sense of trust and confidence in the power of God to see me through, whatever the situation. The story of Jesus was a part of my story, beginning as a young child. Today, every time I read the stories He told, the lessons He taught so long ago, they become fresh and new for me, adding to the story of my life that is still evolving.*

The story of Jesus lives on in the lives of many of the people I have met, and those I haven't, but whose stories inspired me to embrace whatever challenge or opportunity God placed before me. I'm thankful for every encounter and pray that I have been a good steward of their trust as I tell their stories within these pages. I hope I have told their stories accurately while drawing attention to the importance of their faith. You see, the power of the gospel to carry each of us through life's ups and downs becomes the real foundation for our story. As we open up to others, showing them how Christ has made a difference in our struggles as well as our successes, we are able to help them find a stronger path of their own.

While this is true for many today, it was especially true for the early followers of Jesus. His presence, words, actions, and compassion for all people literally changed the world one person at a time. We may not know the details of their lives, but we have benefited from their faithfulness to tell His story, allowing us to catch a glimpse of how He made a difference. There is no more vivid story of Jesus' impact than the one found in the fourth chapter of Acts.

Peter and John were on their way to the Temple for prayers. It was midafternoon and as they walked the familiar road, they must have been talking about all that had happened since Pentecost. What a day that was! It certainly wasn't like any other Jewish feast they had ever experienced. Just as Jesus had instructed, the 11 apostles, His mother Mary, along with His brothers, and some of the other women who had been with Jesus, around 120 in all, had gone to that upper room in Jerusalem and waited. For 40 days since His death, Jesus had appeared to different people in different places. His presence and His message each time had been one of great encouragement and assurance confirming He was alive. The disappointment and grief they all felt after the Crucifixion had turned to anticipation and excitement with each passing day. But on this particular day, on Pentecost, a miracle took place. Without warning, the sound of a mighty wind came rushing into the room and filled the entire house. What appeared to be tongue-shaped fire appeared above everyone in the room and suddenly they began speaking in such a way that people, regardless of their language, could understand what was being said. Those gathered in Jerusalem to celebrate the Feast of Weeks, as Pentecost was also called, heard all the commotion and came to see what was happening. And the rest is history, a pivotal moment in time that changed their lives forever.

Each day the new believers, more than 3,000 of them on Pentecost alone, met for worship and prayer, sharing what was happening in their midst. They followed their tradition of daily worship in the Temple and their numbers were growing. They were learning together what it meant to be a follower of Jesus. They were discovering the meaning of real love for one another and how the love of Jesus led them to a deeper concern for each others' well-being. Yes, life was different, especially for Peter and John, and they all knew it.

*On this particular afternoon as they walked to the Temple, their lives were about to take another new turn. As they approached they saw a lame man, a beggar, being placed at the Temple gate. It wasn't uncommon for those with physical disabilities to come to the Temple to beg. Most hoped that as people went to pray they might be more inclined to help those who were less fortunate. Those who carried them made sure they were placed so as not to be in anyone's way, but unfortunately, that meant they were easily overlooked by the crowd. The spacious porches all around the Temple made it easy for traders, merchants, teachers, and some government and religious leaders to gather and espouse whatever were their views of the events of the day, or sell their wares as people came to the Temple. Again, maybe the Jews, who were following their traditions so faithfully, would have softer hearts and be inclined to spend or give of their wealth.*

*Peter and John were in the crowd that day and maybe in the past they, too, overlooked individuals like the beggar. But today was different. Today they saw him, really saw him, and saw not only his need for healing, but for forgiveness of sin. On this day they stopped and gave him everything they had, faith and healing in the name of Jesus. In an instant his life was turned upside down. Peter took him by the right hand, helped him to his feet, and commanded him to walk. Can you imagine his complete surprise when he realized his feet and ankles had enough strength to even attempt to rise? He may have tentatively, carefully, started to stand at first, but then he knew, not only could he stand, he could walk. So excited with his healing he began to jump and shout and run around the Temple courts praising God. People milling about the courtyard, gathering for prayers, stopped what they were doing to see the cause of all the commotion and in the process experienced the extraordinary. They knew this man. They had seen him at the gate begging many times but they had never seen him walk. They were amazed and filled with wonder and questions. How could this be? What happened to him? Who is responsible? And as he had done on Pentecost, Peter seized the* opportunity to tell them an amazing story, the story of Jesus, the Son of God, crucified and raised from the dead and present with them at that moment through the power of His Holy Spirit. He reminded them of the prophets from the past who had predicted this special One would come and challenged them to see that Jesus was the promised Messiah who could change their lives just as He had healed the beggar in their midst.

Peter and John never made it to prayers that afternoon. In the midst of healing the lame man, teaching and preaching to those who had stopped to witness the miracle, another group gathered. They were less than enthusiastic and had a different agenda than the crowd. The priests, the captain of the Temple guard, and the Sadducees listened while Peter told the story about Jesus being raised from the dead and they became angry. His teaching went against everything they believed. By this time evening was approaching. They knew they had to stop Peter and John from teaching any further about Jesus or performing any other miracles. So they seized them on the spot and took them to jail where they left them overnight. But the story of Jesus had been heard and it had penetrated the hearts of many. Scripture tells us an estimated 5,000 more came to faith in Jesus Christ that day.

The next morning an expanded group of religious leaders gathered to discuss what had happened and what they were going to do with Peter and John. Annas the high priest, Caiaphas, and a host of religious scholars, rulers, and members of the high priest's family were in the group. It was a gathering of the most educated and well versed men in Jewish law, a group that was very concerned about anything that jeopardized their status within the Roman Empire. And before them stood Peter and John, uneducated fishermen from Capernaum; Galileans known for quick tempers, impulsive decision making, and the ability to disrupt the status quo of everyday life. And so they questioned them, tried to intimidate them, and to strike fear in their hearts. But with the amazing courage that Peter had experienced since Pentecost, he began *to share the story of Jesus just as he had with the beggar and all those who witnessed his healing the previous day.*

*The leaders were astounded by what they heard and at a loss for words on how to explain the healing of the lame man. Everyone had seen it take place at the hands of these two ordinary fishermen. As hard as they tried, they realized no law had been broken and were forced to release them, but not without one last stern warning. They were to cease all speaking and teaching in the name of Jesus.*

*And that was that, or so they thought. Without hesitation, Peter and John stood boldly and responded, "Judge for yourselves whether it is right in God's sight to obey you rather than God. For we cannot help speaking about what we have seen and heard" (Acts 4:19–20).*

From where did such boldness come? What was so powerful about the things they had seen and heard that would compel them to keep speaking in the face of great danger? In a short period of time these fishermen had become profound witnesses for Jesus. Their life of ordinary had become extraordinary with the power to heal and perform miracles unlike any they had ever seen. They had moved from being timid, unsure men looking for a ruler to take over the government, to bold proclaimers of the gospel, and everyone on this day knew beyond a shadow of a doubt it was real. Peter and John knew the answer. They had been with Jesus long enough to hear His stories, witness His miracles, and realize He possessed the power of God dwelling within Him unlike anything they had ever known. They knew that by telling His story and allowing God to work through them, they could open the door of any heart for salvation. What was there left to say? The religious rulers threatened them again, but they were without rebuttal on the reality of the healed beggar. So Peter and John were released and they continued to tell the story of Jesus to anyone who would listen.

# Reflections

My story in some ways reflects that of Peter and John. The things I have seen and heard in my own life and in the lives of other followers of Jesus is nothing short of miraculous. Because of Christ's presence living in and through us, I have learned that God is able to change our way of thinking and our way of living. He alone loves us enough to take us from our most broken selves and shape us into people whose lives can make a difference in this world. When we entrust our most personal questions, doubts, and fears to Him, He takes them and turns them into answers filled with hope and confidence that touch the person next to us or on the other side of the world.

My story began at home many years ago. Where does your story begin? Can you echo the words of Peter and John as they declared, "We cannot help speaking about what we have seen and heard" (Acts 4:20)? As we discover and share our stories of faith, we make it possible for His story to live on for the next generation. Our story can become an invitation for others to embrace His wonderful gift of love and forgiveness if we are willing to share.

Section 1    Celebrate

Chapter 1

The Power
of a Story

*W*hat was it that prompted Peter and John to declare so emphatically, "We cannot help speaking about what we have seen and heard" (Acts 4:20)? What did they know so deep in their souls that the trained religious leaders had missed? After all, weren't they the experts in the Old Testament teachings, in the practice of the Jewish faith and all its traditions? Certainly they knew the ins and outs of synagogue life better than anyone else. Peter and John were laypeople, untrained in the Jewish law, and here they were confronting the educationally elite. Peter and John, fishermen by trade, Galileans by birth, what could they possibly know about the kingdom of God that the Sanhedrin did not know?

Knowing about something in your head is not the same as knowing it in your heart. It is not the same as experiencing it. Peter and John knew Jesus; the religious rulers knew about Him. Peter and John had witnessed firsthand the miracles performed by Jesus; others gave lip service to the reports of His actions. Peter and John experienced His death and resurrection and the full range of emotions followed by intense personal transformation as a result of those events. The religious rulers saw the Crucifixion, dismissed the rumors of His resurrection, and went back to life as before convinced that the stories about Jesus were just that, stories that would die away with time.

What they didn't count on was the power behind the story, the personal recounting of a life-changing encounter. The sheer visible difference in a life like Peter's could not be ignored. When post-Pentecost Peter spoke, people suddenly listened because of the dramatic transformation of his personality, his perspective on life, and more importantly, the obvious power he possessed now seen through his actions. Peter had a story to tell and a life that supported the change. The difference between the religious community and Peter, including those who had gathered in the upper room, was power; God at work in and through each person including all those that believed that day. Now they each had a story to tell and, what no one could ever have imagined, telling what happened that day, how their lives were changed, would enable the story of Jesus to live on forever.

## The Parables of Jesus

Coming from a culture that had a rich tradition of storytelling, Jesus used stories to teach many lessons about the kingdom of God. He grew up in the synagogue and therefore knew the stories of faith well and shared them often. But He also told stories using examples from daily life so others could see and understand God's purpose and presence in the world. Parables, as they are often referred to, are simply stories from everyday life with a spiritual or moral truth. There are an estimated 27 different parables recorded in the gospels that Jesus told. It would appear by the sheer volume found in Scripture that story was Jesus' preferred method of teaching.

The disciples recognized Jesus' frequent manner of communicating this way and asked Him one day, "Why do you use stories when you speak to the people?" He responded, "Here is why I use stories when I speak to the people. . . . 'They see, but they don't really see. They hear, but they don't really hear or understand'" (Matthew 13:10–13 NIrV).

Philip Yancey in his book *What's So Amazing About Grace?* says Jesus' parables "were not merely pleasant stories to hold listeners' attention or literary vessels to hold theological truth. They were, in fact, the template of Jesus' life on earth. He was the shepherd who left the safety of the fold for the dark and dangerous night outside. . . . And to those who betrayed him—especially the disciples, who forsook him at his time of greatest need—he responded like a lovesick father."

Jesus wanted to be sure His listeners did not miss the point when He was speaking. He was an extraordinary communicator in part because He was a powerful storyteller. His example laid the foundation for Peter and John who would later boldly declare they could not keep from telling what they had seen and heard so the story of Jesus would live on.

One of my favorite stories from Jesus' teaching is the one that prompted the disciples' question about why He always told stories. Jesus used an example of planting seed, something with which anyone listening to Him that day from the seashore could identify. Many were farmers and planting was a part of their normal routine.

*He told how a farmer went out to scatter his seed and some fell along the walking path, some in rocky places and among thorns, and some in good soil where it produced a great crop. He explained how easy it was for birds to quickly eat the seed along the pathway. He helped them see that where the soil was too shallow among the rocks and the seed was not able to establish deep roots, the plants died before producing anything. He talked about how the seeds planted among thorns would be choked out before the plants could mature. Only the seed planted in good soil would grow and produce the crops they desired.*

*Now He had their attention and He began to relate this story to how people respond when they hear about God's kingdom and faith. He shared how when a person doesn't take the news to heart, it's like the seed on the pathway and Satan easily snatches it away. When the gospel is planted among the rocky places, a person may respond quickly and enthusiastically, but without a foundation to carry him forward he falls away when difficulties surface. The one likened to the thorns is the person who hears the word but allows his worries and the pull of material things to choke out any possibility of faith to take root. Only when the seed is planted in good soil, in the heart of a person who hears it and understands it, will faith take root and grow, ultimately providing guidance for the person throughout life (see Matthew 13).*

Peter and John were in the crowd that day. They saw the reaction of those listening to the story and learned from the very best the power of a story. While nothing anyone could say or do could stop them from telling the story of Jesus in the days following Pentecost, it had not always been that way. Their relationship with Jesus didn't begin with an instant understanding of what they were seeing and hearing. The parable of the seed was as much for them as for those meeting Jesus for the first time. The richness of the soil of their individual hearts for the teachings of Jesus varied from one disciple to the next. It's true they had been with Jesus from the beginning of His ministry, from the moment He called them away from their fishing nets to come and follow Him. But they came with their own expectations. They were part of the culture that longed for the promised Messiah, a ruler that would make life on earth better than it was under Roman rule. They knew the teachings of the Old Testament, made regular visits to the synagogue, and were practicing the Jewish faith as they understood it. But Peter, perhaps more than the others, seemed to have his own ideas about politics and religion and was not afraid to share his ideas with anyone who would listen. Hearing a new viewpoint, a different outcome from what he was looking for was not easy for him. On numerous occasions, even after being with Jesus for some time, he was quick to speak but slow to think and it often got him into trouble.

For instance, one day Jesus came walking on the lake toward the disciples. They were naturally unsure of what they were seeing and afraid, but not Peter. He asked if he could join Jesus on the water. Jesus commanded him to come and he quickly got out of the boat. But then he took his eyes off Jesus and he, too, became afraid. He began to sink and called out to the Lord to save him (Matthew 14:26–30).

On another occasion Peter took Jesus aside and began to argue with Him about what he heard Jesus telling. He insisted it was an inaccurate prediction of His death only to hear Jesus say, "Get behind me, Satan! You are a stumbling block to me; you do not have in mind the things of God, but the things of men" (Matthew 16:23). On more than one occasion Peter spoke first before thinking it through.

Peter and John were part of a select group among the disciples that included James, the brother of John. They had a special relationship with Jesus. Not only had they heard the stories Jesus told but they were with Him on significant occasions when they observed more clearly the true nature of Jesus. They were present when Jesus raised Jairus's daughter from the dead (Mark 5:37). They were with Him when Jesus went to the garden to pray and asked that they watch and pray with Him (Mark 14:33). And they alone were allowed to catch a glimpse of the glory of God with Jesus on the mount of transfiguration (Matthew 17:1).

In three short years, the disciples, especially Peter, John, and James, experienced many things with Jesus. Because of this special bond they were most likely present more often than anyone else to hear the stories and witness the miracles Jesus performed. But they still failed to see the bigger picture of why Jesus came until after the Resurrection.

## The Power Behind the Story

Yes, Peter and John had learned from the very best the power of a story, but it was more than telling a good story that would change the hearts of listeners and ultimately change the world forever. It was the life-changing power behind the story, the reality that God had now come to them, first through Jesus and now through the presence of the promised Holy Spirit, that would enable them to take the story of Jesus beyond Jerusalem to Judea, Samaria, and the uttermost parts of the world (Matthew 28:18–20).

So when the Sanhedrin warned them that day after Pentecost to stop telling the story, they refused; they simply could not go back to their old way of life. What they had once known in their heads they now knew in their hearts. They had experienced the power of Jesus and His resurrection and they were compelled to tell everyone they met. Scripture tells us that Peter and John quickly returned to their people and reported everything that had happened to them. Instead of cowering in fear or wringing their hands wondering what they should do next as they had done in the past, a prayer meeting broke out. They began to celebrate and praise God for all that had happened, even the encounter with the religious leaders. They gave thanks for how His power had been witnessed by so many when the beggar was healed. They prayed for a fresh boldness going forward when they spoke and for power to heal and perform miracles in the name of Jesus. Not exactly what the religious leaders anticipated with their warnings, but it was what Jesus expected when He told them to go to Jerusalem and wait. The Holy Spirit was coming and they would forever be changed. Pentecost had come. The power was there and they could not keep from telling.

Author George Eliot once said, "It is never too late to be what you might have been." I think that's especially true about coming to faith. I'm so thankful for the early influence of my parents and my church. I'm thankful that Jesus has been a part of my life every day since I was eight years old. But I also know that it is never too late to enter into a personal relationship with Jesus as our Lord and Savior. He has and always will be ready and waiting, constantly calling us to come to faith. Knowing about Him is different than knowing Him. When we know Him and respond, no matter our age, a new story begins; one that is life-changing and can be passed on to those who come behind us.

Each one of us has a story. Our life is a collection of experiences that shape and mold us into the people we become. With every passing year our story expands and reflects the choices made in response to life experiences. We share with others the things that help them understand us and know us with more than head knowledge. Sharing our stories helps build relationships that in turn add to the quality of our lives.

It's important to occasionally reflect on our early influences. Looking back often enables us to see the broader scope of how God has interacted in our circumstances. It's a common practice for psychologists to advise their clients to develop a written time line identifying those mileposts, significant events from birth to current day that impacted their lives. What were the critical junctures that prompted some life-altering decision? What unexpected tragedy or surprising joy helped to change a direction? Who along the way altered our path? Discerning those mileposts, in essence, is a way to begin understanding and sharing the story of our lives.

When my husband and I were in the process of being appointed as missionaries, one of our assignments was to write our personal stories. We were given very detailed instructions that included an anticipated length of 20 pages. My first reaction was I hadn't lived long enough to fill up 5 pages much less 20! But as I began to write, as I reflected on those significant life events that had shaped my understanding of who I was and the direction my life seemed to be going, filling up 20 pages was easy. The more I remembered about my early life, the more I saw God's presence and power at work in so many situations. While it took weeks to complete, it was an enriching experience that I wouldn't trade for anything. It gave us a framework for understanding how God was at work in our lives as a couple.

The power of the Holy Spirit to work in a person's heart is an amazing thing. Seeds planted through hearing the stories of missionaries over a period of years helped us see the possibility that God might be calling us to surrender more of our personal will to His desires. Conversations with people who understood the practical side of living in a different culture brought clarity to those areas that seemed cloudy to us. Most of all, asking God to give us a clear vision of His will was paramount. As in the experience of Gideon laying out a fleece before God in Judges 6:36–40, we also placed a fleece before God. We were a jointly called couple and we both felt we offered a unique set of skills for a missions experience. To help us know if this was truly God's call, we requested an assignment from a mission setting that clearly stated a need for a nurse and church planter combination. The day our denomination's mission board called saying the number one need in the Caribbean at that time was for a couple with our exact set of skills we knew in our hearts God had answered our prayers. We said yes without ever having visited the country. The confirmation from the Holy Spirit was the overwhelming sense of peace we both felt with our decision.

Some might think once you reach a decision like ours that you have "arrived" spiritually. Quite the contrary. Some of our greatest challenges were about to begin; physical illnesses for our son, cultural challenges to our faith and long-held beliefs, a lack of recognition of our denomination as a legitimate source for worship in the country, and more. Not long after arriving on the missions field, I began to appreciate the value of going through such an intense time of discerning God's will prior to our appointment, for it is only His call that sustains you when the hard times come your way. I became more grateful for the process and thankful that I nailed down my personal mileposts in the writing of my story. In the years that have followed I have seen how this experience helped me find the words to speak as I share my story with others and in expressing my gratitude to God for all He has done in my life. The more we share the story of our lives and God's power to work through every situation, the greater the possibility we have of helping others experience this same power.

## One Girl's Story of Redemption

*At a youth conference sponsored by WMU, the nonprofit organization I serve as executive director, a young college-age woman, Oksana Nelson,* stood in front of hundreds of teenage girls to tell a story about a girl born in Russia; a young girl whose life had been quite sad and difficult. By the age of eight she found herself living in an orphanage, sharing a room with 3 other girls and a bathroom with 20. Life in the orphanage was far different from that of most children who lived with a real family. Meals consisted of potato soup and other starches with meat only on rare occasions. A bath once every two weeks, a weekly change of clothes, and shared toiletries were the norm. School uniforms and free lunches identified her to the outside world as an orphan, an outcast in Russian society. But school provided a place to learn and a brief reprieve from the reality of her situation. How she longed for a family that would love her and take her away from this life.

On occasion the orphanage allowed visitors to come in and spend time with the children. One group was especially kind, a missions team from the United States. They taught them songs, told stories about a man called Jesus, and even asked if the children would sit with them. Physical contact of a loving nature was a rare thing. One woman in particular asked the girl to sit with her while they passed out gifts, a shoebox filled with things she had never owned. New socks, her own toothbrush and toothpaste, candy unlike any she had ever had, and pictures of the children who had packed the gift box. What a day this had been. But before the group left, they gave her another gift. They told her about a heavenly Father who would never leave her and taught her how to pray to Him.

Believing what she had heard, she prayed. And the first thing she asked for was a family. But by this time she was ten years old, with little hope of being adopted. Or so she thought. In another land far away God was speaking to a family, telling them to seek another child to bring into their family. They had already adopted two and thought they had a complete family. But God had heard a little girl's prayer in Russia and a family in America responded to God's voice.

*When she finished telling the story, she told the teenagers she was the little girl in the story and had been adopted by the American family God had spoken to after she prayed. She reminded them of the importance of allowing their faith to dictate their actions; how something as small as a shoebox of gifts can lead to a miracle when placed in God's hands. As individuals we are called to be faithful in the small promptings of God as well as the things we might think are impossible. Because two children packed a shoebox, a missions team traveled halfway around the world, and a family obeyed when God told them to adopt a child, she now not only has a family but knows the love of a heavenly Father who will never leave her.*

It was obvious by their reaction that Oksana's story touched many young girls sitting in her conference that day. Every time they pack a shoebox or carry gifts to children in a school, or work with children in a homeless shelter they will remember Oksana and the power of a simple gift, a shoebox, when placed in the hands of a committed follower of Christ. I dare say it is a story they will tell over and over as they ponder the ways God wants to use them to tell others about Jesus and His love. The power of one person's story to impact the lives of many was never more real than it was to those present that day.

# Reflections

So what is your story? What are the mileposts that altered your life? Who did you meet along the way that had a direct impact on your decision making? Whose story of God at work in his or her life helped you discover what He could do in yours? Who will you have an impact on with your story of Jesus' love and forgiveness and the difference it has made in your life?

The reality is, we learn from one another as we hear how God changes the circumstances of our lives or gives us the ability to push through whatever comes. Those lessons learned are valuable tools God can use to influence the life of another. Peter and John experienced the power of Jesus to change their lives and they simply could not keep the story to themselves. They had to tell everyone they met and many came to faith.

The Story Lives On

Chapter 2

Reaching
the Generations

*O*n my first trip to the southwestern part of the United States, I was amazed at the vast difference in the landscape compared to the South. Living where trees are in abundance on rolling hills all around me, I was surprised by how far you could see on the open road in the West. The beauty of the red rock configurations and the vastly different colors of the desert were absolutely gorgeous.

In addition to the differences in scenery I was also introduced to a variety of new art forms among the Native American tribes. Beautiful handmade jewelry, pottery, and wood carvings could be found in abundance in shops and open air markets. Another type of art was the Pueblo figurines called storyteller dolls. Helen Cordero is credited with creating the first doll in 1964 in honor of her grandfather who frequently gathered his grandchildren in his lap to tell them stories of Native American culture and tradition. Stories of life among the tribal family passed down from one generation to the next. Looking closely at the clay figurines, children—or listeners as they are often referred to—can be seen resting on the storyteller's arms, clutching their braids, and even perched on the storyteller's back. The greater the number of children, the better the storyteller, we were told. Each one crafted in such a way as to tell a story, a piece of our history, as a part of our American culture that has helped shape our nation today.

Each time I look at my own storyteller figures, treasures from friends in the West, I am reminded of the importance of passing on those things that really matter, the stories of life and faith that make us who we are. In recent years this has become even more important in my role as a grandmother. I want to be sure my two grandsons know their heritage, both in family memories and in matters of faith. As preschoolers they are so inquisitive, wanting to know what life was like when I was a child and even more the stories of their mother when she was their age. Telling the family stories helps them connect with the generations before them, embracing the common values they are being taught today.

When I married into the Lee family, I learned a new appreciation for the importance of family faith stories. My husband, Larry, is an only child and lost his parents before we married. So much of their family history was left for me to learn wherever I could. Thankfully, my husband's uncle, a longtime Baptist minister, loved to sit around the kitchen table after a meal telling stories of the family. I learned a lot about my Larry as a child, some true and some exaggerated, I suspect, from these family mealtimes. But his favorite stories were about his own childhood, stories of people from the different churches he served, and occasionally a story of some quirky family member—twice removed he would assure us.

I was never quite sure how many of the details in his stories were accurate but we loved hearing them. One of his most repeated story lines had to do with "plowing new ground at the home place." With vivid description he relayed the hard work of planting spring crops, harvesting in the late summer, and all the challenges he faced as a child growing up on the farm. You almost found yourself feeling sorry for him as you listened. There was just one problem with his story. As the youngest of 13 children, the family had already moved to the city before he was born. He never lived on the farm, much less "plowed new ground." The stories he told were true but they had been passed down from his older siblings and repeated over and over until they became a part of his own history. So much a part of the fabric of his life, he continued to pass them down to his children and then on to the next generation. The day he passed on to heaven a rich tradition of sharing the Lee family stories disappeared. But, to this day, at the mere mention of the phrase "plowing new ground" a ripple of laughter will begin and we remember.

Passing on the stories of faith is not a new idea. We read in 2 Timothy 1:3–5 where the Apostle Paul reminded young Timothy of his legacy of faith with these words:

*I thank God, whom I serve, as my forefathers did, with a clear conscience, as night and day I constantly remember you in my prayers. Recalling your tears, I long to see you, so that I may be filled with joy. I have been reminded of your sincere faith, which first lived in your grandmother Lois and in your mother Eunice and, I am persuaded, now lives in you also.*

Paul loved Timothy as if he were his own son. He reminded him of his heritage of faith as a word of encouragement for the times he faced adversity and challenges to his faith both inside and outside the church. Timothy's faith began when his grandmother developed a strong faith. She passed it on to her daughter, Eunice, who then passed it on to her son, Timothy. He came from a strong family who embraced the same faith and could draw strength on that fact.

While each person must come to faith individually, the tremendous influence of family cannot be overstated. Parents and grandparents have the potential for the greatest impact on their children for good or bad. While culture, media, and other individuals likewise influence them, children observe how their parents live each day based on what they hear them speak with words. The continuity or disconnection, whichever the case may be, sends many messages about their values and why they make certain choices. Building on what they see and hear within the family provides a framework for their own behavior and decisions. All of our life experiences shape the person we become. Exposing our children and grandchildren to as many good, positive learning environments as possible is critical while they are young.

*Recently my six-year-old grandson was riding down the road with his grandfather when he asked a rather serious question. "Daka (his pet name for his grandfather), what would you do if someone gave you a bucket full of gold coins?" Russell inquired.*

*Realizing that many of their serious conversations take place while he is strapped in a car seat, my husband took a moment to give what he thought was a good answer for a child his age. Then he turned the question back to Russell and asked what he would do.*

*Without hesitation he responded in a rather thoughtful tone, "I would keep one coin for myself and give the rest to my church so more missionaries could be sent."*

What prompts a six-year-old to ask such a question? More importantly, what led him to his answer?

When I think about Russell's experiences so far, I realize his answer came from the things he has been exposed to through his family and the Baptist church he has attended all of his short life. His parents have a missions heart and model that regularly with their actions, involving both of their children in missions projects in the community.

Their church engages members in missions through giving, going on trips, and sharing their stories in worship services when they return. They also believe in the importance of missions education. Russell has attended Mission Friends®, a missions-focused program for preschool-age children, since he could walk into the classroom. On a regular basis he hears the stories of missionaries and the places they serve. At six, he is connecting the dots between what he experiences at church—what he hears in worship as Scripture is read and testimonies shared—with what he is learning at home. He knows that God's love is not just for him, but all the people of the world. He believes he can and should be a part of helping others to know that same love. Just within our three generations faith has been and is being passed down, laying a foundation for the future.

When I think about the stories of other families where multiple generations have followed a strong commitment to living out their faith, I realize there is a common thread. In the midst of busy, often overbooked lives, they still spend quality time together as a family sharing the stories of the past and celebrating the things in life that matter. They pay attention to the small things in life that have a great impact.

## One Family's Story

*Nancy Parris and her family signed up to be a part of a WMU-sponsored missions trip for families. They had purposefully waited until their children would be old enough to go with them. The year arrived and they went to Natchez, Mississippi, where I first met them. It was an exciting week filled with a variety of missions projects. They felt so positive about the week that they made a commitment to go the next year, this time to Cincinnati, Ohio. Following the trip Nancy wrote:*

*We were assigned to do Backyard Bible Clubs and block parties in a housing complex. It was so exciting to see our two children, Sarah and Seth, ages eight and seven, participate with such joy and excitement! They dressed up as clowns and went door to door, boldly inviting children to come to the events. They worked hard helping get ready for crafts, giving out snacks, reading to the little ones, doing puppet skits, and telling as many as they could, "Jesus loves you." Sarah even told several, "We came all the way from Alabama and drove seven and a half hours just to tell you that Jesus loves you!" They worked hard, setting up for the block parties and cleaning up afterwards. Seth even volunteered to take the trash to the dumpster! They took smaller children under their wings and showed them how to play the games during the recreation time. It was such a blessing to be able to serve as a family in such a special way.*

*Parents, grandparents, children, church families are given a special opportunity to serve the Lord side by side. Missions is being taught firsthand to our children. . . . Families are encouraged to be on mission at home, vacation, school, or wherever they may be. We want the best for our children academically. We provide opportunities for them to excel in sports, music, art, etc. . . . What greater opportunity for us to offer our children than the special privilege of teaching them to be all God called them to be—to know Him and make Him known.*

How we live before our children and grandchildren speaks volumes about the priorities of our lives. When they see faith in action each day, they begin to understand the effect Jesus has on our lives and are more open to His power in their own lives.

## Story of Wana Ann and Giles Fort

One family that I have known about for many years but only in recent years have had the privilege of getting to know more personally is Wana Ann and Giles Fort. Missionary parents often face a unique set of parenting issues. With the demands of living in another culture and the responsibility for establishing faith channels with the people you are seeking to reach, time for family, especially children, can escape before you realize it. Children born and raised in another culture often have diverse influences as compared to those raised in only one culture. It would be easy for them to make different choices from their parents. Missionary kids in particular experience a very unusual way of life as compared to others in the United States (US). They face a unique set of difficulties as they decide where they belong. As they return to the US for college they may not feel at home in the American culture. As they seek their own direction professionally and personally, the influence of growing up on the missions field invariably has an effect. It is quite a tribute to the parents when the children develop strong, positive feelings about their experiences, to the point of sensing God's direction down a similar path.

Wana Ann and Giles Fort were the first in their family to surrender to God's call to serve as missionaries. Their story is one of great faith, a complete reliance on the power of God to work through them among people who had never known about Jesus, and to raise five boys, three of whom later followed the same path into career missions. And now a third generation of Fort children is making many of those same choices. What made the difference?

Several years ago at a WMU national event we watched from the audience as three generations of the Fort family gathered in the church to tell their story. It seemed as if we were being allowed to listen in on a great family reunion among parents, children, and grandchildren who loved being together. We listened and for some of us, it was an experience of bringing to life a familiar story learned long ago. One of the first mission studies I remember as a young pastor's wife was the story of Sanyati Hospital and doctors Wana Ann and Giles Fort.

*When they left for southern Africa to serve as medical doctors in Rhodesia (now Zimbabwe), they left behind family and friends that didn't quite understand why two promising medical professionals would give up their bright futures for Africa. Both were well trained and could have had their pick of places to practice medicine and find great success. But theirs was a different calling, a calling to share a ministry of healing connected to the story of Jesus with people who needed both physical and spiritual healing.*

*Wana Ann and Giles were among the pioneers in medical missions. In 1952, when the Forts were appointed, Baptist missions work was only 2 years old in Rhodesia. A church and a school had been started, but the first missionaries realized the need for medical care was urgent. People were dying every day from diseases that were preventable or at least easily treated in many other countries. Working from a small mud and pole building with a tin roof, Wana Ann and Giles began to treat whoever they could while sharing the gospel with all who would listen. Their medical practice was crude and far from what they had known in the US. Life itself was far from easy. Common conveniences, like* clean running water in the home, didn't exist, making even the simplest activity time-consuming and often impossible. For the first 9 years, for instance, all water had to be boiled before it could be used for anything, much less consumed. Laundry was hand done and equipment was lacking at all levels.

But they pressed on, dreaming about the day they would see a hospital, a real hospital providing the level of care the people needed, built at Sanyati. They cast a vision, they prayed, they asked others to pray, and God honored their prayers. For 25 years the hospital grew in its ability to serve the people of Rhodesia and the story of Jesus was proclaimed boldly.

During those years, the Fort family grew to include five boys. As I listened to several of them share about their childhood, I realized that many of their experiences were the same as other children, just in a different place. They attended missions groups, Sunday School, and church regularly and often heard their father preach about the love of Christ. The building wasn't exactly like ours, often a mud hut or under a tree, but the message was the same. They saw their mother, even as a busy doctor in the bush, make time to participate in church activities beyond Sunday worship. Wana Ann had a deep appreciation for WMU in the States so she engaged the women of Rhodesia in the same way, helping them grasp missions concepts and their responsibility to share the stories of Jesus with their neighbors.

The boys grew up moving freely in and out of the hospital and the village where Africans were their best friends, where they were accepted for who they were as children. One of the sons told how their mother after a long day at the hospital still maintained a family ritual of dinner by candlelight on china and linen tablecloths with classical music in the background while the activities of the day were shared.

One thing that was different for the Fort boys was the opportunity to see the commitment of their parents to not only tell about Jesus but demonstrate His love each day through their healing touch as physicians. They saw their sadness when they lost a patient and their *joy when healing took place, especially when a patient expressed faith in Christ. The faith of their parents was never more clearly seen than when their fifth child was born with a disability. The way they demonstrated God's peace in the midst of this challenge on the missions field was something that spoke a tremendous message to the other boys as well as those they served. This kind of faith, so visible and consistent in every way, and the importance they placed on taking time to share all of life together as a family provided a strong foundation that became the story of the Fort family.*

*When Wana Ann and Giles retired after 31 years of service, several of their children had followed in their footsteps in medicine and/or missions. Two sons were medical doctors, one of whom is serving as a missionary today along with two other brothers and their families. Their choices were made with full knowledge of good times and difficult ones. The civil war in Rhodesia that took the life of Archie Dunaway, a much-loved missionary colleague, in 1978 as well as the destruction of the hospital they had witnessed their father build, were painful experiences. Knowing many of their friends were killed during the war had a lasting impact on their lives. But one thing they knew; the One they served was stronger. They witnessed how their parents handled adversity and how God worked in their lives and continues to work in powerful ways today.*

At a recent gathering of Baptist medical professionals, Wana Ann and Giles, now nearing 90 years of age, came to hear their son, Gordon, vice-president for overseas missions of the International Mission Board, speak. They tried to quietly slip into the room but all eyes turned their way when they entered. We all wanted a glimpse of this much-loved couple, heroes of the faith for many of us who have known their story. Their love for missions and missionaries to this day has never waned. And as they pass on this commitment to their grandchildren, a third generation is preparing to follow in their footsteps. What a wonderful legacy of faith for our generation.

## Stories of Sacrifice

Just as the Fort family in the midst of much joy also faced trials and painful experiences during their years of service, some families are called upon to make the ultimate sacrifice for their faith. Missionaries all too often must forfeit personal time with their families to live out their calling. They live in many places around our world that are far less comfortable than what we experience in the United States. In many countries travel, even for short distances, is dangerous due to unsafe roads. Buses and airplanes often are not monitored for safety measures. It is never easy to lose a parent; but when it comes as a result of violence by the people they seek to serve, it is even more painful. It's natural to question why they were taken in such a horrific, painful way. Those are the times when children especially may question their own faith and make life-altering choices, some for good and others less than ideal. It may be years before they fully see God at work in and through the circumstances that brought so much pain.

Years ago I heard author Elisabeth Elliot speak about faith and following God's call no matter what the situation. Through tragic circumstances she and four other wives had lost their husbands and experienced the amazing grace of God in the midst of their tragedy. Their story has become a testimony for countless numbers of people around the world. Understanding the motivation for service when sacrifice is called for can often help those close to the person gain better insight.

A journal entry written by Elisabeth's husband, missionary Jim Elliot, prior to his death in Ecuador provides a glimpse into the passion of one man for sharing what he had experienced in his own life as a follower of Jesus: "He is no fool who gives what he cannot keep to gain that which he cannot lose." Perhaps Elliot was thinking about the Scripture from Matthew 16:24–25 (NKJV) where Jesus said:

*"If anyone desires to come after Me, let him deny himself, and take up his cross, and follow Me. For whoever desires to save his life will lose it, but whoever loses his life for My sake will find it. For what profit is it to a man if he gains the whole world, and loses his own soul?"*

Maybe Jim Elliot had a sense that he might pay a personal sacrifice to accomplish that which he knew deep in his heart God was calling him to embrace.

*Jim Elliot's call to missions came after much soul-searching while attending Wheaton College. Having been raised in a Christian home in Portland, Oregon, he was influenced early by his parents and church attendance, making a profession of faith at age six. That commitment sustained him well through school years and in 1945 he left Oregon for college in Illinois. At Wheaton, like many of his classmates, he participated in missions conferences and even spent one summer as a student missionary in Mexico. He was seeking direction for his future and chose people and places that would help him gain understanding. At one of the Intervarsity Student Conventions held during those days he felt God's call to work with tribal people in Central America. This thought helped focus his studies and he began to study languages, including Greek. After meeting a former missionary to the Quechua people, he had the opportunity to practice writing languages under his guidance. It was during that time that he first heard of the Waorani people, or the Auca, as they were often called; a violent tribal, unreached people in Ecuador.*

By 1952 he and his fellow missionary Pete Fleming were off to Ecuador to work with the Quechua people, but always with the Waorani tribe in the back of his mind. Jim and fellow missionaries Pete Fleming, Ed McCully, Roger Youderian, and pilot Nate Saint recognized the risk involved in taking the gospel to people like the Waorani who had never heard; but they knew God was calling and they moved forward.

The five men began to reach out to the tribe by flying over their village and dropping gift baskets while surveying the area. At one point they camped at a nearby stream and met one of the tribesmen. Not knowing that the person they perceived as friendly returned to the tribe and lied about the purposes of the men, their best efforts were cut short. On January 8, 1956, all five men were killed by a group from the tribe who didn't know the real purpose behind the men coming to their village. When they failed to communicate with their families at an appointed time, a search began. The bodies of the five were later recovered along with some of their personal effects, including Jim Elliot's journal with the entry, "He is no fool who gives what he cannot keep to gain that which he cannot lose."

Leaving behind five widows and nine children, the possibilities of fulfilling the calling heard so long ago as a student among the Waorani seemed impossible. But God's desire to be known even among this violent tribe never waned. Through much grace and forgiveness the widows of the slain missionaries committed to reach the tribe with the gospel. Sometime following their deaths Nate's sister, Rachel, and Elisabeth, Jim's wife, actually lived among the people, sharing the story of Jesus while helping establish a Christian community. All of the children were left to seek answers to their own questions, but in time the seeming waste of life gave way to a bigger picture of God's hand in bringing healing and salvation to the very people their fathers sought to save. The only difference was it came through the faithfulness of their mothers and other family members.

*One of the nine children, Steve Saint, son of pilot Nate Saint, later wrote about the impact of his father's life and death in an article for Christianity Today. Now a husband and father himself, he and his family moved to Ecuador in 1995 to work with the very people who killed his father.*

*My father and his four friends were not given the privilege of watching their children and grandchildren grow up. I've often wished I could have known my dad as an adult, for Mom and Aunt Rachel have often said our thought processes and mannerisms are much alike. I have trouble distinguishing what I actually "remember" of him and what I have been told. But I do know that he left me a legacy, and the challenge now is for me to pass it on to my children. Dad strove to find out what life really is. He found identity, purpose, and fulfillment in being obedient to God's call. He tried it, tested it, and committed himself to it. I know that the risk he took, which resulted in his death and consequently his separation from his family, he took not to satisfy his own need for adventure or fame, but in obedience to what he believed was God's directive to him. I suppose he is best known because he died for his faith, but the legacy he left his children was his willingness first to live for his faith.*

What no one could have imagined was the impact the story of these five brave men would have on future generations. Their story of giving their lives for people they did not know lives on today, inspiring generations of young people to follow God's call to missions. But even more, the incredible story of forgiveness among the wives and children teaches us much about the magnitude of God's grace in ways we could never have understood without their story.

In recent years, Baptist missionaries have once again given the ultimate sacrifice for their faith.

*Dr. Martha Myers was killed along with two other hospital staff members, administrator William Koehn and purchasing manager Kathleen Gariety, in Yemen in 2002. A Muslim extremist entered the hospital where they served and shot them.*

*While each of these were loved and respected by many, the loss of Martha Myers, who had served at Jibla Baptist Hospital for more than 25 years, was especially painful for those of us who knew her personally. She had grown up through the missions organizations that are a part of WMU where I serve today. She was a frequent speaker at missions events when she was home in Alabama and her stories inspired many other young girls to consider the possibility that God might be calling them to be doctors and possibly missionaries. In her quiet, loving way she touched the lives of so many women and children in Yemen who lacked adequate health care. Always giving her best as a doctor, she also gave them what she loved most, the story of Jesus and how He could bring healing in ways she could not. Inscribed on her gravestone in Yemen where she was buried are three simple but powerful words—She Loves God. Seeing how she lived each day, how she emulated the life of her Savior was a tremendous testimony to those who observed her life. Martha may not be with us physically today, but her story lives on in the lives of those she touched and those who will hear her story for years to come.*

# Reflections

If we were to create our own storyteller doll today, what would he or she look like? Would there be children clutching our braids and perched on our backs anxious to hear the stories of our lives? Or would we be sitting alone without a story to tell? Where are you on your journey of faith—at the very beginning or have you accumulated many stories of how God has led you? With faith comes our own unique and important legacy to pass on to future generations. Our story is special to our families. But when our story is also a tribute to the faithfulness of God in all aspects of our lives, the story becomes much bigger and makes a difference in the lives of those who will come behind us.

Chapter 3

The Art of
Storytelling

*A*uthor Claudia Royal in her book *Storytelling* says, "Storytelling is an art, just as music, sculpture, or painting is an art. . . . The storyteller creates a word-picture—a work of art. . . . The story may be defined as a series of events, so related as to form a connected whole, and told in such a way that it moves the will to right action."

Jesus understood the importance of using stories to lead people to faith. He was a master at creating word pictures to which everyone could relate. For instance, in Luke 15, Jesus presents three stories that emphasize the worth of every individual person to the kingdom of God. He tells of a shepherd who loses one of his 100 sheep, a woman who loses one of her ten silver coins, and a father who loses one of his sons. Each character in the story is unique. They respond to their loss in a personal way, searching diligently until they find it. The spirit of jubilation over the recovery of each item is clear. At the end of the first parable Jesus says there is "more rejoicing in heaven over one sinner who repents than over ninety-nine righteous persons who do not repent" (v. 7). He repeats the essence of that fact at the conclusion of the parable of the lost coin. When He tells the story of the father who finds the son who was lost, He goes a bit further, explaining to the disgruntled son who had never left home, "We had to celebrate and be glad, because this brother of yours was dead and is alive again; he was lost and is found" (Luke 15:32).

The progression of the stories, the descriptions of the search, and the emotions surrounding the finding of what had been lost are presented in such a way that it made an impact on the listeners then as it also touches our hearts today. We are captivated by how

He communicates the depth of love of our heavenly Father for each of us, even when we wander away, and how He longs for us to return. Henri Nouwen wrote,

*"God rejoices. Not because the problems of the world have been solved, not because all human pain and suffering have come to an end, nor because thousands of people have been converted and are now praising him for his goodness. No, God rejoices because one of his children who was lost has been found."*

Storytelling is truly an art. The power of words to tell the story of Jesus cannot be overestimated. As we follow Peter and John throughout the Book of Acts, Luke helps us see how the story of Jesus' life, death, and resurrection changed individual lives and cultures, and birthed the church. But it required courage on the part of the apostles and other believers to keep telling the story in the face of persecution and growing hostility.

In Acts 10, Luke tells about the time when Peter faced a crucial moment in his faith journey and as a leader of the early church. The question of whether or not the gospel was for all people, the Gentiles in particular, came to the forefront. He experienced a vision from God and without hesitation he embraced the opportunity to go to Cornelius, a centurion, and tell the story of Jesus. As a result he witnessed many who were present come to faith. His defense of the gospel, the power of God's love to embrace all people, was never more significant. Because of Peter, the possibility for me, a Gentile, to come to faith 2,000 years later was set in motion.

Luke was a wonderful storyteller. As a physician, his eye for detail is evident in the way he recounts the experiences of the disciples and the early church. Good storytellers know how to pick their words just as an artist knows the right colors for the canvas.

They both paint a picture that enables a person to see, touch, and feel the characters. When a story is told in such a way that it can be remembered and applied to everyday life, attitudes and perspectives often change. As we grow in our faith, our personal story becomes a tool that God can use to help others on their journey.

## Storytelling by Radio

Stories are delivered in a variety of ways, but one of the most common ways, aside from print, is through listening. An ever-increasing avenue for "reading" in our fast-paced world is to listen to audiobooks while driving our car or from our MP3 players as we walk or fly or wherever we are. It reminds me of days gone by when radio was the primary source of communication. I have images as a young child of my grandparents sitting in the living room on the farm after a long day listening to the news and then to some popular radio personality of their day.

A familiar sight in St. Vincent during the 1980s when I served as a missionary was people walking up and down the mountainous terrain of the island with a radio sitting on their shoulder. Booming music or the voice of a favorite broadcaster from a nearby island could be heard at all hours of the day or night. It was the primary way of keeping up with happenings where they lived and in the region. The radio in St. Vincent also proved to be a source of embarrassment for me one day when we left our three-year-old son watching the planes come and go at the airport as we gathered students from our church to take them home. I thought his father had him, he thought I did. Only when we arrived at our destination did we realize he was missing. Panic-stricken, I raced back to the airport only to find him laughing, sitting on the wall outside the airport with all the cab drivers. They said they knew I would come back for him so they entertained him by feeding him peanuts!

Matthew loved the small airport, which we could see from our front porch. He would stand for hours watching and announcing when the planes arrived on the short landing strip. Living as close as we did to the airport, we were often the ones sent to pick up visitors or nationals returning home to the island and he always wanted to go along. It was a place where he was happy and therefore unafraid on this particular day. Once I started driving home, for a fleeting moment, I hoped no one would know how distracted we were and what a horrible thing I had allowed to happen. But that hope lasted only a few minutes. When I pulled into the driveway I was greeted by neighbors who asked if I had found Matt. When I asked how they knew he was missing, they said they heard it over the radio. Like I said, radio was the way to know everything that happened on the island.

During this same time frame, radio was popular among many in the United States, whether listening to National Public Radio for discussions on the latest news events, sharing personal viewpoints on talk radio, or listening to the occasional program where you were entertained by a great storyteller. Radio has endured the test of time as a source of communication. Paul Harvey made telling stories by radio exciting with his famous phrase "now, for the rest of the story." You knew something worthwhile was about to be expressed that made the story even more important than what you had just heard.

*A Prairie Home Companion* debuted in 1974 as a type of variety show on the radio before a live audience. The most popular segment for many years seemed to be the weekly monologue by its creator, Garrison Keillor, called "The News from Lake Wobegon." Based on a fictional town "where all the women are strong, all the men are good looking, and all the children are above average," listeners were captivated by the characters portrayed in his stories. You were left with the feeling that he was talking about someone you knew in your own town or met somewhere in your past. The stories made you laugh or cry or pause to think about your own situation. One of my husband's favorite radio shows was *Tinyburg Tales*. It was not uncommon for Larry to wake up the family early on a Sunday morning to come to the den and listen to the latest happenings from Tinyburg. I can't say that the children were especially thrilled with his decision but they still laugh whenever Tinyburg is mentioned after all these years.

*Created by the late Robert J. Hastings, his stories were based on a fictional small town that was home to a variety of churchgoers, civic-minded individuals, kids, and mischievous pets. Many of the stories were especially amusing and often reminded you of individuals in your own church. But Tinyburg was a bit different than Lake Wobegon. Bob Hastings placed his own twist on the Lake Wobegon description when he described Tinyburg this way:*

***It's a place where you know everyone, yet still get along. It's where the men are strong, the women good looking, and all the children above average. . . . It's a place where every problem has a happy ending. It's a spot we want to hold on to come what may. It's Tinyburg, thirty-five miles from Bigtown and the nearest interstate highway and just seven miles south of Pretense. Easy to find, hard to leave. Elusive. Receding into yesterday. Too precious to give up, too good to be true.***

*He reminds us that when you enter Tinyburg the sign says: "Welcome to Tinyburg: the only city in the United States with an unlisted zip code." Buried in the humor of his stories was always a truth about the basic goodness in people that left you with something positive to think about and possible ideas for handling similar situations. Much of his material came from his 55 years as a minister and personal experiences growing up in a close-knit community. He knew Baptist life well and could speak to church issues in a subtle way with creativity and much credibility. As a graduate of Southwestern Baptist Theological Seminary and editor of the Illinois Baptist newspaper from 1968 to 1984 and author of several books, he was a much-sought-after speaker for church settings and as a teacher at writers conferences. After leaving the paper, he spent much of his remaining years as the creator and primary storyteller of Tinyburg Tales on the Bible Broadcasting Network. He influenced the thinking of a broad population with his use of the story based on Christian teachings.*

Radio is also a valuable tool for crossing cultural barriers with the gospel into places that are not open to a Christian presence. When people hear the stories of Jesus, their hearts are often softened and become more receptive to accepting the gospel.

In recent years WMU has partnered with a wonderful organization in Jordan. Called Arab Woman Today (AWT), this is another story about where we have seen the power of storytelling for sharing the gospel.

*Their leader is an incredible woman of great vision and commitment who states her purpose is "to see the Arab woman reconciled with God, herself, and society." They provide a number of training events each year, networking opportunities for women of common background and need, printed resources, and a Web site where information is shared freely. While many Arab women are highly educated and have access to the Internet, an equally high percentage cannot read and have few opportunities to hear the stories of the Bible. Radio became an important avenue for reaching out to this population and storytelling was the chosen vehicle.*

*For 11 years, AWT has remained faithful to their commitment to reach this untouched audience by producing a 15-minute radio broadcast called* Woman Today *addressing problems faced by Arab women in their families and society. It is a costly venture for the small ministry. Through a partnership with Trans World Radio the program is edited, recorded, and aired twice a week across 22 countries in North Africa and the Middle East. Through drama and a brief, biblically based message that follows the story, women are discovering ways to cope with their problems while hearing the truths of the gospel. God has performed an amazing miracle through the lives of many who have heard the broadcasts.*

For many who cannot read, listening to stories of Jesus told in their native language is the only avenue to come to faith. Radio, recorders with messages, and other tools for sharing the gospel orally are a part of keeping the story alive, allowing it to touch the hearts of people around the world.

# Storytelling Through the Arts

The power of a story does not rest with the printed or spoken word alone. Stories that are presented visually can often communicate in ways beyond the spoken word. My refrigerator, like many of yours, I suspect, has always been the place for family communication. Reminders of dental appointments, music lessons, and meetings in the midst of a variety of souvenir magnets covered the front and side open to the kitchen. When the children were young, it was where special artwork or spelling tests with an A+ were displayed. You could tell a lot about our family activities just by looking at the refrigerator.

Time passed and Matt and Allison moved away to college, leaving fewer special items to place on the refrigerator. It seemed bare for a while and boring no matter what I added. But that didn't last long. Today there is little open space. Every inch is covered with a picture painted by Bennett or the early writing efforts of Russell, special messages from my young grandsons to their Nana. I love watching the progress being made by both as they learn the art of drawing and writing.

My daughter's refrigerator is now filled with these same types of mementos and messages. Bennett and Russell are both bringing home pictures and school notes that are beginning to find their place. Not long ago she noticed Russell had a real flair for art and seemed to be enjoying his kindergarten art class. Almost in passing one day he said one of his pictures was going to be at the museum and then off he went. Later one of his friends said, "Russell, did you tell your mom your picture was going to hang in the museum one day?" And again he nodded and off he went. It wasn't until she received a letter from his school announcing that Russell had painted a picture called *Picasso's Funny Face* and it had been selected for a special children's showing at the local museum did she realize this was for real. His class had been studying Picasso and of all the kindergarten student entries his had been chosen. It was a special day when we gathered with all the other proud parents and grandparents. The children's artwork was framed and hanging in the main gallery. Refreshments and music, special certificates and words of praise were heaped on the children in a wonderful way. For a child who needed to find expression for his feelings outside of words, Russell has certainly found his niche for now. His art communicates his feelings and experiences that are a part of what will become his personal story.

While art is often a personal expression of how we feel or some emotion that is seeking an outlet, it can also be used to tell the stories of the Bible.

*In Atlanta, Georgia, missionaries Kerry and Twyla Jackson are using their gift for art to draw other artists together for faith discussions. Their ministry is called Drawing to the Rock, and through it the Jacksons are building relationships with other artists. They display various paintings at shows, use creative painting during presentations that tell the story of Jesus, and are available to discuss the questions that many in the art community have about faith. Christian artists like the Jacksons understand the importance of reaching out to those who share a common lifestyle like the arts which serves as an entry point for discipleship.*

A friend of mine recently used her gift for painting during a WMU-sponsored national event for teenagers.

*Rianna Freeman, a talented young artist, painted on large canvases during the worship sessions of the event. The teenage girls were spellbound by her work, which helped hold their attention while the stories from Scripture were being spoken. Later when she conducted art classes in breakout sessions, the girls were sitting on the floor outside the room waiting for their turn to learn more about using art in ministry.*

Another example of the use of art in telling the stories of the Bible is the impact of stained-glass windows found in many churches.

*My own church setting provides numerous stories of Jesus beautifully depicted around the sanctuary in vivid colors of glass. In quiet moments before the beginning of worship I find myself studying and remembering the biblical account of Jesus at His birth, death, and resurrection. I see Him gathering the children, carrying the lost sheep, knocking on the door, and the stories of the Bible suddenly come alive with visuals that I might not have grasped from the printed or spoken word alone.*

*Several years ago I attended a church in another state where their sanctuary was adorned with several of the most exquisite stained-glass windows I had ever seen. The pastor is a friend from years ago that I had not seen since he came to this church. His message that day was presented through music as he played the piano, led us in singing hymns of faith, and telling the story behind each of the windows. It was one of the most profound worship experiences I have ever been a part of with all the visual and sensory aspects of worship. I was reminded that we all "hear" the stories of Jesus in many different ways and all are acceptable in His sight when offered for His glory.*

As executive director of WMU, I have had the privilege of traveling to many places outside the United States. My husband and I love to find the out-of-the-way places off the tourist map to explore and discover what life is like for the average person. We eat in small cafés and walk through local grocery stores to gain an understanding of the economy. We take public transportation whenever possible to experience their most familiar way of travel. One of our favorite things to do, especially when in Europe, is to explore the cathedrals and churches in whatever town or city we visit. There is so much history and religious understanding that comes from a quiet walk around the grounds and inside the churches when they are open.

Sometimes I've felt great sadness when it seems the church is only a museum and has lost its reason for existence. At other times it is encouraging to see how they are reaching out to a new generation with creative approaches that I might not have considered. Always there are those with beautiful stained-glass windows and ornate paintings on the walls and in the ceilings telling biblical stories while reminding us about the sacrifice Jesus made for each of us. In many instances these visuals, just works of art to some, might be the only glimpse of Christ people see since some will never enter the church for worship. It does, however, become an entry point for the gospel through hearing or reading the story behind the art.

On one of our trips to England we took the train to Coventry to experience this historic city but also to visit the Cathedral of Coventry, which was bombed by Germany on November 14, 1940, during World War II.

*Much of the cathedral was destroyed, leaving only a few walls standing. Shortly after the bombing a stonemason examining the damage noticed two fallen roof timbers had landed in the shape of a cross. It became a symbol of hope amidst the devastation and was later placed near one of the remaining walls of the fallen sanctuary where the words* Father Forgive *were still legible. A month later on Christmas Day, the provost of the cathedral made a commitment over a national radio broadcast to seek a bridge to forgiveness and reconciliation instead of revenge. He publicly declared he would work with those who had been their enemies "to build a kinder, more Christlike world," casting a moral and prophetic vision that reshaped Coventry, the nation of England, and beyond as it continues as a voice for peace today.*

*But the story doesn't end there. As we walked around the ruins, read the printed guide that gave us reminders of the history of this place, we came upon a bronze statue that took our breath. Two individuals on their knees were leaning across what appeared to be a great divide in a touching embrace. The word* Reconciliation *printed across the plaque beneath it said it all. Some who have visited Coventry have commented it became a holy moment for them, a place where they encountered God for the first time. I certainly stood in awe, quietly soaking in the meaning of this statue in the midst of what was left after a senseless war. I became keenly aware that only God could speak to the tragedy of that day and bring good from*

*The Story Lives On*

*evil. This statue hinted at the possibility of forgiveness and the cathedral gave evidence of the One who would provide the healing.*

*Josefina de Vasconcellos, an English sculptor whose father was Brazilian, created the original statue after the war. Her original thought was to symbolize the reuniting of two individuals kneeling over barbed wire in an embrace and named it* Reunion. *A very compelling emotion felt by so many right after the war, she and others soon realized it had a far greater significance beyond the individual. At the age of 90, she recreated the statue without the barbed wire and renamed it* Reconciliation, *symbolizing the possibility of two nations reuniting in forgiveness. In 1995, Richard Branson funded and donated the current replica to the cathedral in Coventry. For all of those who promised reconciliation instead of revenge it stands as a symbol of hope and a reminder of what is possible when we allow God to speak into our situations. A duplicate statue was also created and placed in the peace gardens of Hiroshima by the people of Coventry. A symbol of forgiveness on the part of two nations has forged an international movement of seeking reconciliation in many other parts of our troubled world. The story of reconciliation is a powerful one when we realize Christ has paid the price for our own forgiveness and pleads with us to do the same for others.*

Seeing, reading, and hearing the stories of Jesus are an important part of our growth and maturity as followers of Christ. When words are combined with art—visual presentations of things like stained-glass windows, painted walls and ceilings, or a perfectly sculpted statue—a picture of faith that is life-changing emerges and we catch a more complete picture of the One who makes all of life worthwhile.

Peter and John heard the stories of Jesus, not over a radio or a recorder, but from the lips of the Master Himself. They saw the truth of His stories lived out in the way He touched people. They faithfully told the stories after He was gone once they realized the significance of His life, death, and resurrection. They sensed that if the story of His sacrificial love was to live on, it was up to them to keep telling the story and demonstrating the power behind the story. Just as Peter opened the doors of faith for Cornelius and his household, you and I can do the same today for those we meet. The way we tell the stories of Jesus may vary. Some will be through words, others through art, music, and more. Whatever method is used, a credible witness of the impact Jesus has had on our lives can be told.

# Reflections

What kind of storyteller are you? The number one fear identified on numerous surveys is the fear of public speaking. Maybe you are someone that finds it difficult to put your experiences into words. Do you have a gift for painting, sculpting, or music? Maybe you love to quilt or design stained glass. How can you use your artistic talent to tell your story of faith and keep the stories of Jesus alive for another generation?

As we embrace the forgiveness and love of Jesus, we soon realize we have a story of our own to tell the world. We know the difference He has made in the way we handle the challenges of everyday life, how we react under pressure, and when difficulties arise. We recognize where to turn to receive encouragement when we fail and power to get up and try again. It's in telling these stories with whatever means at our disposal that we find a reason to celebrate God's blessings and the courage to face the next day allowing others to be inspired to follow the same path, the way of Calvary where peace and forgiveness are waiting.

Section 2

Connect

Chapter 4

Stories of
"the Least of
These"

*I*'ve always been a doer. I have friends who love to sit and debate politics, sports, and theology. They get all excited analyzing the pros and cons of the latest technology, what's wrong with their boss, or how they feel about the latest issue at church. While some of them are activists and will seek resolution or change, most of them just love the debate. I can take just so much debate and then I want to go fix it. I think that desire is part of the reason I became a nurse. Nurses are generally doers. If we stood over your hospital bed and only debated the pros and cons of the latest prescribed treatment, you might never get well. Good nurses analyze quickly and then act.

As followers of Christ, I recognize there is a time to study, debate Scripture, and even argue over approaches for reaching people with the gospel; but eventually there comes a point where the debate stops and we are called to action. The stories of Jesus are packed with significance. He faced questions and even debate at times over His teaching, but He also acted when He was confronted with a need. Always the teacher, He used those instances to instruct those who might be watching and listening. Not only did He bring clarity to issues people were facing about everyday life, He provided insight into how He wanted all of His followers to live.

Equipping the disciples was especially important. Above all others they had to understand the purpose of God in the world and the role Jesus played in fulfilling that purpose. In Luke 4 Jesus began teaching using Scripture that provided the clearest statement of why He came. He quoted verses from Isaiah 61:

*"The Spirit of the Lord is on me, because he has anointed me to preach good news*

*to the poor. He has sent me to proclaim freedom for the prisoners and recovery of sight for the blind, to release the oppressed, to proclaim the year of the Lord's favor"* (Luke 4:18–19).

From the moment He called each of the disciples they witnessed how He lived out this purpose. He spent a great deal of time during His earthly ministry preaching, teaching, healing, meeting physical needs, and preparing the disciples for leadership. Matthew 9 tells us,

*Jesus went through all the towns and villages, teaching in their synagogues, preaching the good news of the kingdom and healing every disease and sickness. When he saw the crowds, he had compassion on them, because they were harassed and helpless, like sheep without a shepherd. Then he said to his disciples, "The harvest is plentiful but the workers are few. Ask the Lord of the harvest, therefore, to send out workers into his harvest field"* (Matthew 9:35–38).

He never asked the disciples to do anything He was unwilling to do. His teaching was often followed by some demonstration of healing or performing a miracle. Then He would send them out to put into practice what the Scripture taught.

On one occasion He was asked when the end of the age would come. Always looking for the opportunity to teach more than what might have been asked, Jesus responded with a story. A portion of the Matthew 25 passage is a litany of words that reminds us how Jesus served others. As His disciples today, it provides a word picture of who we are to serve, how we are to serve, and the spirit with which we are to serve as well.

*"'Come, you who are blessed by my Father; take your inheritance, the kingdom prepared for you since the creation of the world. For I was hungry and you gave me something to eat, I was thirsty and you gave me something to drink, I was a*

*stranger and you invited me in, I needed clothes and you clothed me, I was sick and you looked after me, I was in prison and you came to visit me.' Then the righteous will answer him, 'Lord, when did we see you hungry and feed you, or thirsty and give you something to drink? When did we see you a stranger and invite you in, or needing clothes and clothe you? When did we see you sick or in prison and go to visit you?' The King will reply, 'I tell you the truth, whatever you did for one of the least of these brothers of mine, you did for me'"* (Matthew 25:34–40).

Because of their growing understanding of and personal experiences with Jesus, the disciples knew the value of following His instructions. The more they saw Him heal, forgive, and challenge the status quo, the more they sought to emulate His actions. The teaching of Jesus in Matthew 25 is just as relevant and challenging today as it was when first spoken. The power of the gospel story lives on because of the way it was lived out by those who followed Christ first. Generation after generation of believers have continued to demonstrate God's power to heal and forgive by giving of themselves—their resources, talents, professional skills—placing all they have into God's hands to touch the lives of hurting people. When we allow God to step into our circumstances, He can do incredible things to bring about complete healing, physically and spiritually, so life can be lived wholly in step with His will.

*"For I was hungry and you gave me something to eat."*
*(Matthew 25:35)*

During the first few weeks of living on the island of St. Vincent in the Windward Islands, our family had many adjustments. Life was a mixture of establishing living patterns for the family and learning my role as a missionary nurse in this new place. Two years prior to our arrival another family had settled into the country, researched the medical needs, and identified the places where nurses could address some of them. Medical care was limited, but a small hospital existed for basic needs. It wasn't long before we understood that many children's health issues were clearly linked to malnutrition and lack of adequate sanitation.

*My immediate assignment was to help launch classes in the villages where women would be taught basic nutrition and cleanliness to help prevent more serious, long-term health problems. Vitamin A deficiencies, for instance, were widespread. So a first step was to provide instructions on how to plant a small kitchen garden utilizing seeds for green leafy vegetables. Another problem was protein deficiencies, so baby chickens were distributed at the end of the ten weeks to those who completed the course. The chickens would provide the eggs needed for young children who were facing poor growth and development due to this missing ingredient in their diet.*

*Over the course of several weeks it was wonderful to see the trust level grow. People in the villages, sensing our genuine concern for their families, began to open up about other needs. They were curious about why American nurses were living in their country when we could be practicing in the United States. What made us care about them and their needs enough to leave our families and plant our lives in their situation? They eventually opened up about spiritual issues as well. As we shared about Jesus and prayed with them, the door would open to start a church in their village where others could hear the stories of the Bible.*

Connecting the story of Jesus with actions that met basic needs affirmed the importance of what Jesus taught the disciples. "I was hungry and you gave me something to eat" was a way of telling them "God loves you." And it was more than just a handout; we were teaching them to feed their families for a lifetime because Jesus cared about them.

My experience in St. Vincent is not unique. All around the world the needs of individuals for food and water, basic health care, and a place to live, when connected to the life-changing story of Jesus, results in changed lives. Matthew 25 provides the framework for how we are to serve in Jesus' name so He can perform this great work.

## Taylor and Susan Field and Graffiti Ministries

*On a visit to New York City in 1993, I was introduced to a place called Graffiti Center. Established in 1974 as a ministry outreach to the people living in New York's Lower East Side, Graffiti had a long tradition of feeding the homeless, hosting Bible studies, and working with the children living in this highly diverse area. The name Graffiti describes the appearance of the center. When a group of college students from Alabama volunteered to help make this storefront property suitable for ministry, they found that every time they painted over the gang graffiti on the walls it would reappear. So they decided to create their own with more appropriate words and designs depicting the impact Christ would have on this community. The name Graffiti stuck despite many efforts through the years to change it.*

*Taylor and Susan Field serve as career missionaries, pastor, director, counselor, and mentor to the people of this community and the hundreds of volunteers who pass through these doors. They met in New York during a summer urban missions experience not long after Graffiti began. A seed was planted in both of their hearts, for each other, and for the people of Lower East Side. Years later, after more formal education, marriage, two children, two years of service in Hong Kong, and Taylor completing a PhD from Golden Gate Baptist Theological Seminary, they knew God was calling them back to New York to urban missions. By this time Graffiti was well established in its ministry role, but it was time for a church to be planted in the midst of this very diverse culture. In 1986, Taylor and Susan accepted the challenge, moved into a small apartment near the center, and began what has become a lifelong commitment for serving "the least of these" of New York.*

*The first few years were spent getting acquainted with the neighborhood, planting seeds of friendship and trust through afterschool tutoring, Vacation Bible Schools, Wednesday night Bible studies, and offering food and clothing to the homeless that lived in the park near Graffiti. The work was hard, discouraging at times, with seemingly few positive long-term results. But they continued to serve in whatever way they could find. One of their approaches was to host a brown-bag day in the park. Around noon one day a week the staff and volunteers would take peanut butter sandwiches, or whatever they might have in the pantry that day, and head to the park. They called it F.L.I.P. for short—free lunch in the park. The bags were given away as conversations were started and relationships built in hopes of finding a more sustainable way to live. This demonstration of concern for their physical hunger opened doors for addressing their spiritual hunger as well.*

*Arthur was one of those who came for a sandwich one day. His emotional distress was quite evident; and as he poured out his heart, Taylor learned his story. Arthur lost his job, which led to frequent bouts of drinking. He eventually lost his family, house, and car—everything he owned—and was now on the streets. He was sobbing and Taylor wondered what had set off this kind of emotion while standing in line for a sandwich. One of the volunteers, Arthur said, had spoken a kind word and given him a sense of dignity he had not felt for some time. He showed Taylor a book and pamphlet he was reading, the Bible and a witnessing tract. He asked if Taylor believed what was written in the Bible, and after a short conversation Arthur prayed to receive Christ.*

*Weeks after regularly attending Wednesday night Bible study, soaking in all he could about his new faith, Arthur disappeared. Time passed and one day he called to confess that on the day he met Taylor he failed to tell him he had escaped from prison. He felt as a believer he needed to make that right. He turned himself in and was in prison, but he assured Taylor he was continuing to share his faith. He wanted the Graffiti family to pray for a young man to whom he was witnessing and he promised to pray for the outreach programs at Graffiti. Over the next six months he called periodically to report on other inmates who were listening to his story of faith and how four of them, now believers, were having Bible study together. How amazing to see God at work in Arthur's life even while in prison.*

*Arthur completed his prison sentence and found a job in northern New York working in a Christian ministry. He called one day to give Taylor an update on his life and asked if he remembered how all this started, eventually leading him into ministry following prison. Taylor asked if it was something said at the Bible study he attended or when his cell mates professed Christ. The answer was simply no—it was when the man in the park said a kind word as he gave him a peanut butter and jelly sandwich. It melted his heart and allowed the words Taylor spoke that day to bring faith and healing for Arthur's physical and spiritual needs.*

Taylor and Susan, as well as others who serve at Graffiti, understand the connection between meeting immediate physical needs and the words we use as we minister in hopes of sharing the message of God's love. They demonstrate this love every day as they listen to the stories of the people on the streets of Lower East Side and point them to the eternal truths found only through Jesus. "I was hungry and you gave me something to eat" is more than a lesson Jesus taught, it is the model which we all are to follow.

All across the world people each day must face a lack of the basic necessities of life—food, clothing, and shelter. While the economic outlook seems discouraging to many of us, it has become a life-and-death issue for others. Human services stretched beyond capacity, continued high unemployment, and rising fuel costs leading to higher food prices are having a significant impact on everyone trying to help those in need.

ACCORDING TO A RECENT HUNGER REPORT:

1. THERE ARE 1.02 BILLION PEOPLE IN THE WORLD WHO DO NOT HAVE ENOUGH TO EAT.

2. EVERY DAY, ALMOST 16,000 CHILDREN DIE FROM HUNGER-RELATED CAUSES—THAT IS 1 CHILD EVERY FIVE SECONDS.

3. IN 2008, NEARLY 3 MILLION CHILDREN DIED BEFORE THEY REACHED THEIR FIFTH BIRTHDAY DUE DIRECTLY OR INDIRECTLY TO HUNGER AND MALNUTRITION.

4. IN THE US, 49 MILLION PEOPLE STRUGGLE WITH HUNGER, INCLUDING 17 MILLION CHILDREN.

5. AN ESTIMATED 35 PERCENT OF POOR FAMILIES IN THE US ARE FORCED TO CHOOSE BETWEEN BUYING FOOD AND PAYING THEIR RENT OR MORTGAGE.

6. IN AMERICA'S CITIES, 1 IN EVERY 4 PEOPLE IN A SOUP KITCHEN LINE IS A CHILD.

# We Can Care

The problem seems so big we often wonder if we can make a difference. We can. It begins with educating ourselves about the reality of hunger and offering to help the ministries who are making a difference. Local food banks, church food pantries, and mission centers usually have the infrastructure and the expertise to address long-term and short-term hunger needs. They often need willing hands to help collect, pack, and distribute food boxes. If we can't give our time, we can provide financial assistance to help them alleviate the pain of hunger.

It's not enough to tell a hungry person that God loves them; we must show them by helping solve the causes of their hunger. Likewise, it is not enough to solve their hunger issue and fail to tell them about God's love. Our actions and our words go hand in hand as we tell the stories of Jesus. Working together we can make a difference in feeding hungry people, and when our help is connected to the life-changing story of Jesus, the results have an eternal impact.

*"I was thirsty and you gave me something to drink"*
*(Matthew 25:35).*

Have you ever been really thirsty? So thirsty you thought you would die if you did not find something to drink? Or maybe you found yourself in a place where water was everywhere but you knew you couldn't drink it because it wasn't safe. One of the basic training guidelines for missions teams going overseas is to know when and where you can drink the water. I have served on several medical teams through the years where the water was so dangerous that even brushing your teeth with it would make you sick. On one particular team to a remote place in Brazil I knew the danger and was so careful all week. I used only bottled water, refrained from ice in all my drinks, and never ate anything that I had not personally peeled or was certain had been thoroughly cooked. On the trip home we had to overnight in a hotel in a large city. I thought the worst was behind me and even though the coffee that morning was only lukewarm I drank it. By the time I landed on American soil, I was terribly ill with a type of dysentery I had tried so hard to avoid. The coffee water had not reached a safe temperature and I was now paying for it.

In many places around our world those who live under these conditions on a daily basis are losing their battle for health due to waterborne disease. In addition, long-term parched land is forcing people to leave their homes and travel on dangerous roads across thousands of miles, all in search of this most life-sustaining ingredient—water. Something as simple as turning on the tap in our kitchen is an often-overlooked blessing. We trust that when we pour water into a glass and drink it we are safe. Unfortunately, that is not the case for so many in our world.

The World Health Organization and related research groups estimate "the number of people who do not have any form of improved water supply facility stands at 1.1 billion globally. The number of people without basic sanitation is 2.4 billion." Most of the populations without access to adequate drinking water and enough water to sustain the growth of food are in Africa and Asia. Without a reliable source of water, many preventable diseases become life threatening and food supply evaporates as well. Poverty increases, famines emerge, and the death of so many innocent people become the statistics you and I read about every day in the newspaper.

"This is terrible," we say, "but what can I do?" Others may even respond with "Why should I care? It's not happening where I live." While there are many reasons we should care, one of the most overwhelming reasons for me as a Christian is because Jesus cared. He made the issue of thirst and water the subject of several stories in addition to Matthew 25. One of those is found in John 4 when Jesus encountered the Samaritan woman at the well.

*Jesus had been traveling with the disciples. After arriving in the town, the disciples left Him to go in search of food. It was probably a hot, dusty day and it makes sense that Jesus was also thirsty. Water was not as easily accessible for travelers as it is today. You had to have a bucket to draw water and a utensil to drink from once you found a well. Since Jesus was traveling He most likely had neither. But as He came upon the well, He met a woman who did have a bucket and was in the process of drawing water. Their encounter began with a request for water.*

*Being fully human, Jesus understood what it was like to feel thirsty. He probably knew the painful condition of someone becoming dehydrated. Water is essential for life. Without it a person becomes critically ill quickly with headaches, nausea, vomiting, and if not resolved soon, coma and death. In this conversation Jesus equated physical dehydration, a painful experience for one who is thirsty, with spiritual dehydration.*

**"Everyone who drinks this water will be thirsty again, but whoever drinks the water I give him will never thirst. Indeed, the water I give him will become in him a spring of water welling up to eternal life" (John 4:13–14).**

*The woman was spiritually thirsty and obviously seeking to quench her* thirst in all the wrong places. Just as today, many experiencing spiritual thirst try to quench it with alcohol, drugs, and all forms of immorality only to discover the thirst continues. She was seeking it through relationships with men, those who were her husband and those who were not. By the time their conversation was over, her thirst had been satisfied and she rushed to the townspeople to tell them about the one who "told me everything I ever did" (v. 39).

This isn't the last time Jesus used water to teach us about eternal life. Later in John 19 we read His final words, "I am thirsty," as He faced death. When He took the wine vinegar drink offered through a sponge, Jesus said, "It is finished." He took the bitter cup of sin on Himself so we could experience eternal quenching of thirst once and for all (John 19:28–30).

Water is the one thing we can't live without. It is the only thing that fully satisfies our thirst. Drinking from the water that Jesus offers likewise is the only thing that fully satisfies our spiritual thirst. No one said following Jesus would be safe, or easy, or simple, but He does provide the only lasting solution to the thirst of our souls.

Helping individuals and communities find solutions for a lack of clean, pure water opens doors for sharing the love of Christ in ways we may never imagine.

# Pure Water, Pure Love

*In the year 2000, WMU began planning targeted missions efforts around the United States with local groups of caring believers. As these groups identified the needs in their communities, we would work alongside them to develop a plan for how volunteers could assist them with hands-on projects. In 2005, WMU partnered with fellow Baptists in San Diego for just such an event. Leaders in the area told us about their ongoing work across the border in an area of Tijuana, Mexico, where people were living without adequate food, water, shelter, and health care. Many of them were refugees from Central American countries who reached the border thinking they could find a better life in the United States and for a variety of reasons could not cross over. Most had nothing to return home to after hurricanes, earthquakes, and other natural disasters had taken everything they owned. Life had become unbearable and they sought a way out, only to find themselves living in an area where the trash was deposited, a no-man's-land, a place where they became invisible. More than 7,000 people took refuge in this place and began to build whatever kind of shelter they could from discarded materials.*

*Once we learned about their plight, we knew something had to be done. The situation was unacceptable and we committed to work together to resolve whatever problems we could. The most important issue was the lack of clean drinking water readily available for the people. Through a special grant from Pure Water, Pure Love$^{SM}$ (PWPL), a WMU-managed fund designated for providing clean water, a new water system was built inside Centro Shalom Alamar, the only church in the area which also serves as a community center. The people felt comfortable accepting free water from the center because they knew the people who worked there cared about them. At the same time they were hearing about God's love through the stories of the Bible that were being shared. The water containers themselves carried a sticker that said "Jesus loves you,"* *making a connection between the life-giving water of Jesus and the physical care of His followers. What a joy to stand with others who care about the people of Colonial Alamar and fill jugs of water, who offer free medical care and food for the people living in this place. It gave new meaning to Jesus' words, "I was thirsty and you gave me something to drink."*

*Recently a young couple and their children visited our offices to share their success story of how access to clean water had changed the lives of the people they work with in a country in North Africa. In a remote mountain region the people lived without access to clean water, creating a serious hardship for their families. It was a part of their daily routine to walk long distances, collect the water in large containers, and carry it back home. Through a WMU PWPL grant, engineers and volunteers were able to locate a water source far beneath the earth's surface. The day the well was drilled and they saw water bursting forth was a day they said no one would ever forget. The joy on the faces of the people in the pictures we saw brought joy to ours as well. This simple act of kindness and generosity has now opened the door for our friends to connect the stories of Jesus, who provides living water, with the physical water provided by people they didn't know but who cared about their need.*

Jesus told the disciples, "The harvest is plentiful but the workers are few" (Matthew 9:37). When we meet a need for food or water for one who cannot do it for themselves, we have ministered to Him; we have become one of the much-needed workers. As much as I want to be the one constantly on the front line, always giving the food or water, the nurse who fixes things, I realize that is not always possible. But that doesn't relieve me of the responsibility to care.

When I can't go, I still need to look for solutions. Can I provide the resources so someone else can go? Do I have the knowledge or access to solutions that I can share with others? Are there ways I can influence the system that makes hunger and disease so prevalent in an area and maybe make a difference?

# Reflections

Where do you see hungry people in your town? Are there places where you would be afraid to drink the water due to poor sanitation or the discoloration of the water from a fountain or tap? Who could you partner with to meet the needs of those in your midst who hunger and thirst physically and spiritually?

When we work together to serve and find solutions, our reach goes much farther around the world. Together we are responding to the call for workers to work in the harvest, and at the same time ministering to Jesus because we minister to the least of His children.

Chapter 5

Stories
That
Challenge
Us

"I was a stranger and you invited me in, I needed clothes and you clothed me" (Matthew 25:35–36).

*S*itting in front of me in church were two young men that seemed new to our congregation. After the service I walked over to introduce myself and discovered they were natives of Afghanistan living and working in my hometown. As we talked, I realized I had heard about them long before this encounter. A friend told me about meeting two Afghani young men when she stopped by a local shopping center after a meeting we were both attending. While she knew only a little of their story, she was intrigued and wanted to keep in touch. A retired couple in our church had invited them to their home for dinner and a friendship had emerged. And on this day the young men had agreed to attend worship with them. As the weeks passed by, others we knew reached out to them as well and we learned more of their incredible story.

*Jamal and Jamshed came to the United States after a heartwrenching journey crossing many countries over the span of 20 years. After civil war broke out in their homeland, their father snuck them and numerous others to safety in Pakistan in the back of a truck. A year later they moved on to Iran in hopes of finding relief from the constant persecution. Life was calmer for a time but it became obvious that they were not welcomed as foreigners in Iran for the long term. Sensing increasing unsettledness, when the boys were 13 and 14, their father once again arranged for them to leave, this time without family or friends.*

*After a treacherous experience recounted in a book titled* Chasing Hope, *their guide abandoned them in Germany. Alone in a strange land, unable to communicate, they wondered what to do next. What they didn't* realize was this would turn out to be the place where God would intervene and lead them to a new family and ultimately to faith. Rescued from the streets, they were initially placed in a children's home by the police. Life improved somewhat. They had a safe place to sleep, food to eat, and a way to attend school. Through their relationships at school they met the mother of a classmate; she reminded them of their own mother still in Iran. The family invited them into their home for meals and soon became friends. Sensing that God wanted them to be a part of the boys' lives in a more permanent way, the family sought permission to adopt them. They were missionaries from the United States living in Germany so the government would allow them only to serve as foster parents. But that was enough to give the boys hope. A new life began for all of them as they learned what it meant to be family together.

In 2001, the boys came with their new family to the United States for the first time for a visit. Several months after arriving, the bombing of the twin towers in New York took place. They witnessed the tragedy unfold on television and heard the discord emerge from multiple fronts. While they had heard many times about the God their foster parents worshipped, Jamal and Jamshed were still Muslim. But this experience led them to question their beliefs and they began to read the Bible for themselves. Two months later they called their father to tell him they were now followers of Jesus Christ and, with his blessing, they were baptized. Returning to Germany as a family, they settled into a new routine that was soon interrupted. Their new family would be transferred back to the United States permanently. But what about the boys? After much prayer, red tape, and ultimately God's intervention, the boys were granted a six-month visa that would allow them to live in the US with their foster parents. Knowing the serious danger that exists when someone of Muslim background embraces Christianity, the family sought asylum status for the boys, hoping they would be allowed to remain in America permanently.

*Jamal and Jamshed, now in their mid-20s, have a new life. They live and work in a place far away from the war they knew as children. They pray that one day their Afghani family can know this same physical peace as well as the spiritual peace that comes from knowing Jesus personally. They have learned to trust God with their circumstances, especially the uncertainty of gaining permanent US acceptance. They know firsthand the importance of following Christ every day because they have experienced what can happen when the teaching of Matthew 25 is put into practice. They were strangers in many different places, but God provided a family that invited them in. All around us are strangers waiting for someone to care, to show them kindness, and to teach them the way just as Jesus taught the disciples.*

Have you ever been a stranger in a foreign land? Have you experienced moving to a new place where you did not know anyone? It can be a frightening time unless someone invites you into a friendship, a caring relationship, where you can learn the ropes and the culture of your new home.

## My First Week as a Missionary

*I will never forget the first week my family lived in St. Vincent, Windward Islands. We were new missionaries moving with two young children to a place we had never seen. Thankfully, another missionary family had preceded us and welcomed us with open arms. They showed us how to find our way through the West Indian system of currency, banking, and shopping in a market where you were expected to barter for the food you wanted. They taught us how to drive on the left-hand side of the road sitting in the right front seat of the car. (Now that was an experience none of us want to repeat.) They became wonderful co-workers and friends as we shared in the work we were all called to do.*

*When my husband became the pastor of a church in the capital city, the Vincentian people welcomed us as well. They helped us meet the community around the church, learn their approach to worship, which included steel pans and choruses that were new to us. They were patient and kind and allowed us room to grow in our new homeland. We faced our share of other people outside the church who were not so kind, some who were anti-American or just not welcoming of any strangers to their country. Those experiences helped us appreciate our Christian friends even more and made us keenly aware of our responsibility to reach out to those who were new to us and our community in the future.*

Sometimes welcoming the stranger is not always positive at first. Initial conversation may lead to discovering the worst side of humanity. As we open ourselves up to hear the stories of those we meet, we might find the needed response will challenge us to our core. They may have endured persecution, hatred, abuse, and the wounds are deep. As we try to engage them in a friendship, we must be willing to listen to their story, hear their pain, and accept them where they are as we also look for a way to minister to them. But through it all, we each learn new viewpoints and new cultural awareness that enrich our lives.

# A Voice for Change

*One of the most popular movies in recent years is* Amazing Grace. *It is the story of two men who met Christ and as a result were forced to face one of the great injustices of their day. William Wilberforce was born into a wealthy merchant's family in the 1700s and lived a rather self-centered life. He made friends with the wealthy and powerful while in college and at the age of 21 was elected to the British parliament. An aunt tried to steer him in the direction of religion through the Methodist Church, but he was uninterested even to the point of ridiculing those that did believe in God. But one day he met Jesus and his life took a dramatic turn. He committed his life to Christ and soon realized God was calling him to open his eyes and heart to something that was accepted as a normal part of the culture of England. At one point he met John Newton, a man who had once been a leader in the slave-trading world, now turned believer in Jesus Christ; the author of the profound words of the hymn, "Amazing Grace."*

*With Newton's urging, Wilberforce began to lobby for changes that would impact the culture and daily lives of those involved in slavery. His decision and subsequent actions in his role in the British parliament sent a ripple effect around the entire world. After many attempts, slavery was declared illegal. Those who had once been invisible to the average person were now in full view.*

*John Newton and William Wilberforce, two very different men, embraced faith in Jesus Christ and experienced a radical departure from the way they had previously viewed their own society. They were compelled by the gospel to see the stranger in their midst, the person sold into slavery, and seek a far-reaching solution. By their actions, their courage, they changed England and the world forever.*

While the actions of men and women like these have made a difference in many places, slavery unfortunately continues in a variety of forms today. In recent years the personal stories of individuals sold into slavery, prostitution, or trafficked illegally for labor have come to light. Modern-day John Newtons and William Wilberforces have also risen to the occasion to advocate for the rights of individuals to live their lives freely without the oppression of others dictating their choices.

## Human Exploitation Today

*Human exploitation* has been defined as the unethical, selfish use of human beings as a means to an end for the satisfaction of personal desires and/or profitable advantage. This kind of selfishness often begins early in life through childhood bullying on the playground, harassing others over the phone and through email, and today over text messaging. It can be seen in the growing problems of pornography, forced labor through illegal immigration, and even human trafficking. Numerous television shows in recent days have delivered a story line based on the alarming problem of young girls from many countries being taken away from their families and sold into prostitution and slavery. Sometimes, human trafficking is initiated by their families due to the ravages of poverty. I read about a ten-year-old girl named Gita who was sold into a brothel by an aunt. Years later she told of being held down by the other girls so a "customer" could rape her because she refused to work. Out of that experience her life changed dramatically and she later became HIV-positive. A life wasted because of the greed of another.

In its broadest definition, *human trafficking* means the commerce and trade of people, legal or illegal, for modern-day slavery, forced labor, and servitude. In other words, it is our modern-day version of slavery. Some researchers have estimated as many as 27 million adults, of which 80 percent are female, and 13 million children around the world are victims of human trafficking. Approximately 30,000 victims a year die from the abuse, disease, torture, or neglect associated with being trafficked.

Why should we care about these issues when it doesn't hurt us personally? The writer of Proverbs challenges us to "speak up for those who cannot speak for themselves, for the rights of all who are destitute. Speak up and judge fairly; defend the rights of the poor and needy" (Proverbs 31:8–9). We must recognize the realities of today and seek to discover redemptive solutions so we, too, might end slavery in our day as John Newton and William Wilberforce did in theirs.

## Ginger's Story

*Ginger Smith is one of those seeking solutions. Serving as the executive director for the Mission Centers of Houston (MCH) she discovered the reality of slavery in her own backyard. I first met Ginger when she lived and worked in New Orleans, Louisiana, at Brantley Baptist Center, a shelter for homeless and drug-addicted individuals. Her experiences in New Orleans laid the foundation for all she would face after moving to Texas. Ginger came to Houston building on the ministry of great leaders who had served the centers prior to her arrival.*

*One of the most beloved missionaries early in my years of missions awareness was Mildred McWhorter. Known for her uncanny ability to tell the stories of those she met at the centers, Mildred brought attention to* the needs of the inner city in a way that others could see themselves working with her. Generations of "critters," as she lovingly called her summer missionaries, can testify today to the life lessons learned from working with Mildred. Ginger is carrying on that same tradition today. Leading the ministry of three Baptist centers in three different areas of Houston presents many challenges, but the relationships and success stories also bring much joy.

Sitting over beignets one evening in New Orleans, I listened as Ginger and Kay Bennett, a New Orleans missionary serving in the same type of ministry, compared their approaches to helping raise awareness of the needs of as well as minister to the people in their communities. I asked each of them, "When did you first become aware of the issue of human trafficking within your neighborhood?"

With three locations in Houston's inner city, Mission Centers of Houston is always looking for opportunities to minister to people in need. Although we've grown accustomed to seeing prostitution, drug abuse, and violence, it wasn't until 2009 when we discovered the very real issue of human trafficking in our community. I remember seeing billboards along Interstate 10 in Houston that advertised the abolitionist movement for the end to modern-day slavery. I'd never heard that term, yet was immersed with this language over the next few weeks. The words were on billboards, in coffee shops, and on TV commercials.

During this discovery period, I found myself in a conversation with two other MCH staff members. Without any previous conversation about modern-day slavery, we started to share our concerns of some questionable activities in our neighborhood. One person shared about a local cantina that he heard sold girls for $2. One shared about a raid at a local bar where they suspected underage girls were being sold for sex. I shared about the massive amount of exposure to publicity *that I had experienced. We decided we had to do something. The pieces started falling in place.*

Ginger and her staff learned about an educational meeting that would be held at a local church to discuss the issues regarding modern-day slavery the next week and they attended. Assuming most of the faith community was in the same situation as they were, "uninformed but concerned," they decided to host a series of luncheons to educate those who would listen. They began to work with a local coalition (Coalition Against Human Trafficking in Houston [CAHT]) trying to educate themselves as well as others. A local ministry group formed, but in the end they realized that while they now had a lot of information, they still didn't know how to help make an impact on the problem. Ginger had been in ministry long enough working with churches to realize many have well-meaning people that want to help but are not professionally trained to deal with trauma victims, much less girls who had been trafficked. She was deeply concerned about the average layperson going into brothels or attempting to rescue women from these types of situations. After hearing stories of ill-equipped people trying to help, Ginger said she and her staff decided to find ways to support law enforcement and work within their parameters. Working together she believed they could make an impact in Houston.

*The Coalition Against Human Trafficking in Houston connected us with the Women's Center in Houston. The Women's Center works directly with the FBI to provide emergency resources to rescued victims of sex trafficking. When asked how we could help, they suggested we collect sweat suits, underclothes, flip-flops, and snack items. These items would be accessible to FBI agents who are investigating and rescuing women.*

*When law enforcement raids a cantina or brothel, they often arrest everyone who appears to be involved in prostitution. It's the only legal way to forcibly remove someone against their will. If they didn't arrest them, the removal would be kidnapping. They often believe the women may be victims instead of perpetrators.*

*Instead of taking them to jail or some other place that will further victimize them, they take the women to a safe facility like a hotel for questioning. They'll often block off a series of rooms and keep the women there for 24 to 78 hours while they interview them.*

*During this time, the women have only the clothes that they were rescued in. Law enforcement says that the women are constantly squirming and preoccupied with "covering" themselves. The sweat suits are baggy and provide good cover and a sense of safety during these interviews.*

*We also believe our ministry is as much to law enforcement and first responders as it is to the women. The FBI has said they are grateful for the NGOs (nongovernment organizations) that provide these resources because their budgets do not allow it.*

Ginger and the staff of Mission Centers of Houston have made a commitment to continue to raise awareness among the churches about the issues and discover ways they can partner to meet the needs of those hurt by human trafficking. They serve on a variety of community response networks seeking a common pathway to rid their city of this human tragedy. It will take courage to stay the course and boldness to stand up when they are challenged. They have a much clearer understanding of the words of the writer of Proverbs when he said: "Speak up for those who cannot speak for themselves, for the rights of all who are destitute."

# Kay's Story

*Likewise, in New Orleans, Kay Bennett, the director of Baptist Friendship House, a ministry for homeless women and children, has also faced the issue of human trafficking as well as the broader issues of human exploitation. I've heard her stories many times of the impoverished women who have walked through her doors, some finding success and others not willing or able to complete all that is required to discover physical and spiritual healing. Aside from the poverty that exists in New Orleans, before and even more so after Hurricane Katrina, the exploiting of individuals, especially women and children, is a growing problem. In a recent letter Kay shared the following story:*

*Providing homeless ministry for 24 years in New Orleans at Brantley Baptist Center and now Baptist Friendship House has on many occasions brought me face-to-face with the horrible issue of human trafficking. Human trafficking has always existed though the term is fairly new and it has become a billion dollar industry. New Orleans has seen an increase in human trafficking, especially post–Hurricanes Katrina and Rita. Providing homeless ministry naturally lends itself to minister to human-trafficking victims. Those who survive trafficking often find themselves homeless.*

*After learning of WMU's Project HELPSM emphasis on human exploitation, I began to research and God began to open my eyes to how big the problem is of human trafficking. I read of how the FBI ranks the Interstate 10 corridor as the highest trafficking corridor in the US. I was then told by a friend who provides trafficking ministry on the Gulf Coast of how thousands of children are brought in through the ports along the Gulf Coast and placed on trailers of 18-wheelers then taken across I-10 and other interstates to be placed in climate control storage units, rural barns, and other places to be photographed for pornography and to be sold.*

*To know that children are being photographed and sold for sex led me to the only conclusion possible; something must be done. God placed a desire in my heart to create some type of ministry along the I-10 corridor to combat human trafficking. God also sent another missionary, Kendall Wolz, with the same desire to work alongside me. Together we researched, attended trainings, advocated, and educated others on the issue of human trafficking.*

While Kay's education and passion were growing, it wasn't until she and Kendall were on their way to a speaking engagement in Florida that it all became more personal.

*We decided we would prayerdrive to Florida along the I-10 corridor. I have driven I-10 numerous times in my life, but I have never driven it with the intent of taking a close look at how human trafficking can occur along an interstate. I had thoughts run through my mind such as* **What should I be looking for?** *and* **What am I not seeing?** *The thoughts led to emotions from the realization that women and children could possibly be in the back of some of the trucks we passed. As I drove I thought,* **What if it was my child in the back of the truck, what would I do?** *I quickly realized it is someone's child and that is all that matters. The emotion became so strong at one time that I could literally imagine a child being in the back of a truck screaming, "Will someone please help me!"*

*The statistics are overwhelming and I thought,* **How will we make a difference?** *Then I realized we make a difference one at a time. If it was my child and someone rescued him or her, it would matter to me.*

Kay went on to say:

*Trafficking does not only occur from victims being transported in the back of 18-wheeler trailers, it occurs in the cabs of trucks. Truckers often pick up children, teenagers, and women at truck stops or along their routes for sex. Statistics show that one-third of runaways are lured into prostitution within 48 hours of leaving home. Driving along I-10 we saw billboards advertising adult stores, adult videos, and adult clubs. Traps set to lure truckers into dark places where the travesties of life will take place and choices will be made that will have lasting consequences. The ride along I-10 not only opened my eyes but opened my heart. The only logical conclusion I came to is that if I really believe this is happening, and I do, then I must do something.*

## Having a Radical Impact

One of the results that both Ginger and Kay experienced after all the research and education was the realization that if they could gather the best resources and people together to address the issue, they could have a more far-reaching impact.

Today a coalition of concerned individuals and ministries has emerged with the specific goal of targeting the I-10 corridor which runs from California to Florida. The group that Kay has organized will look for ways to address the issues along the Gulf Coast from Texas to Florida. Kay believes they can find ways to assist victims and decrease the existence of human trafficking on the I-10 corridor by working together. She also believes out of their experiences will come a model for ministry that can be replicated on all the interstates throughout the United States creating a presence that, as Kay puts it, "will not only make it uncomfortable and hard for trafficking to occur, but will eventually make it virtually impossible for it to occur."

So what can we do? A beginning point for all of us is to see if our states have laws that prohibit human trafficking. In my own situation I was shocked when I learned it was not against the law to traffic a girl in Alabama until recently. The legislature had refused to see the issue and respond to a plea for action until the news reported a major sting operation on a group regularly bringing girls across the state line. It had gone on for some time because we did not have a law making it illegal. It was the fastest response to an issue suddenly made public that I had ever seen in Alabama. The legislature passed a law within three months. But at this writing, still not every state has taken this step on behalf of innocent victims.

We can also begin or join efforts in our communities to minister to victims. Providing food, clothing, and hygiene items to assist law enforcement might be a need. If you have a battered women's shelter, often they are the ones called upon to help and could receive donations. Transportation might be needed for the victim to see a doctor or seek legal advice. It begins with an assessment of your own community, what is available and what is needed. Most of all we can pray, asking God to bring light to this dark issue. Ask Him to open our eyes and help us see the need and how He wants us to respond. When I asked Kay why we seem to be so slow in addressing these issues, she had an interesting observation and challenge.

*As I have watched many organizations tackle this issue only to see statistics increase, I have wondered what is missing.*

*The truth is Satan loves to keep things in the dark. Most people are content not to listen to many organizations and to think they are making something bigger than it is just to get government or grant money. On the other hand, when Christians, through faith-based ministries, start speaking up and bring into the light what has been in the dark, people take notice because God is at work and it is God who prompts people's hearts to take action. Therefore, it is God at work that will make a change and make a difference, not an organization, but God's army. A Christian presence that not only talks about an issue but takes action against the issue creates a climate of change. When we pray, we must be willing to give our prayers feet and take it to the street. In this case, take it to the big street, the interstate.*

As I write this story, training for a group of interested ministry leaders along the I-10 corridor has begun. It is a beginning point for putting feet to our prayers. Kay remarked, "Needless to say, human trafficking ministry is intense." Our goal? To begin Turning Highways into Lifeways.

The night of conversation over beignets was a night I won't soon forget. Just before meeting me at Café Du Monde, Kay had been searching for a missing girl from Friendship House, one she was convinced had been taken from the street and was in one of the adult clubs in New Orleans.

# Reflections

What will be our response to the victims hiding just out of sight as we travel I-10 or whatever interstate passes through our town? Will we close our eyes and look past the motels and adult clubs in our own city?

Or will we open our eyes and our hearts asking for direction and wisdom from our heavenly Father, who sees it all and has taught us to love the stranger, care for the weak and the needy despite their circumstances?

Jesus said, "I was a stranger and you invited me in, I needed clothes and you clothed me."

Chapter 6

Stories
That
Empower
Us

*"I was sick and you looked after me" (Matthew 25:36).*

*The Story Lives On*

*T*he stories of medical missionaries have always held a great fascination for me. Maybe that's true of all nurses who have served on missions teams or short-term missions assignments. For me it began with the first missionary I ever met. I was a freshman nursing student and she had just completed her service in the Middle East as a journeyman, a two-year program for college graduates under the age of 26. Her stories of what it was like during the turbulent years in Gaza during the 1960s were beyond anything I had ever heard. The diseases and challenges of treating those with injuries inflicted by guns and homemade bombs were not a part of my training at the Baptist Hospital. Most of all, I think I was captivated by the idea that a single girl would leave the United States to serve in a hospital that far away. I had never traveled west of the Mississippi River, much less outside the United States. What would drive a person to do something like that? The idea of missions in general was new for me, let alone international missions. But this single encounter planted a seed that God nurtured and one day resulted in my own appointment as a career missionary nurse, outside my country, and ultimately as a volunteer to many other places around the world.

Throughout the New Testament we frequently read stories of Jesus demonstrating compassion and healing for people with physical illnesses. In Matthew 9 He healed a woman with a bleeding problem and in Luke 13 one who was unable to stand up straight. He healed a blind beggar (Luke 18) and the paralyzed man at the pool of Bethesda (John 5). Jesus taught by His example that meeting a person's physical need often removed barriers to hearing the full redemptive story of healing that comes through faith.

# Brief History of Medical Missions

Meeting physical needs as a part of missions emerged as a result of the lack of quality medical care in many places where missionaries served. As early as 1730, history records physicians traveling to places like India and China to establish medical care. Some died soon after arriving for a variety of reasons, but that did not deter the continued desire of physicians, followers of Christ, to meet the physical as well as the spiritual needs of people.

Medical missions among Baptists finds its beginnings in 1846 when J. Sexton James was appointed to China. Unfortunately, he and his wife drowned before they could begin their work. Others followed, but not until 1893 did medical missions really take root. After the turn of the century, hospitals built in China and Nigeria became avenues for health-care ministry that proved valuable in sharing the message of Christ. The stories of Jessie Pettigrew, the first missionary nurse appointed in 1901, and later Dr. Bill Wallace, both of whom served in China, added to the validation of medicine as a point of service for missionaries that imitated the healing touch of Christ.

For many physicians, nurses, and other medical personnel, missions was a natural part of their professional calling and their personal lives as Christian believers. But it was not easy. Life in the bush of Africa and in the tropical climates of Asia and South America proved difficult as they faced diseases unknown in the American medical system. In the midst of all the challenges, however, there are incredible stories of God at work performing miracles that far exceeded anything they had ever seen. When they returned home on leave, the stories they told inspired one generation after another to risk everything to be a part of the healing process in foreign lands while sharing the message of Christ.

# The Story of One Missionary Nurse

Mary Saunders was one of those risk takers. Born in Charleston, South Carolina, in 1923, Mary dreamed of becoming a nurse. Her parents wanted her to follow their path and work for the railroad but she refused. Unhappy with her decision, they told her she would have to pay her own way to college. Having accepted Christ as her Savior at the age of 13, she began a journey of discovering God's plan for her life, one founded on prayer and personal commitment. She enrolled in the Roper School of Nursing, working her way through school, studying when she could, and staffing the hospital to satisfy the requirements for her training.

During her senior year, life changed dramatically with the bombing of Pearl Harbor. Nurses were soon in short supply, especially in the military. With her brothers involved in the war, she felt she, too, should do her part and joined the army. She served well, but life as an army nurse was lonely and difficult. She drifted as a follower of Christ for a time, unsure of where her life was heading. One day word of her mother's illness came, forcing her to return home. Reconnecting with her church and Duna, the woman who led her to the Lord and mentored her through the early years of her faith, Mary began in earnest to seek God's direction for her life again. Before long she heard His voice clearly and announced to her church that she felt called to go to Africa as a missionary nurse. Little did she know how long it would be before that call would become reality. It was a journey with many ups and downs, including marriage to a young man, who, though wonderful, was not called to missions. She never lost sight of how God was leading through her work in nursing and her marriage. She trusted He would work it out for His good in His timing and God did just that.

In 1951, Mary and Davis Saunders were appointed as missionaries to Africa, first to Nigeria, then Kenya, Tanzania, and Zimbabwe. Regardless of the town they lived in or the official job her husband was assigned, Mary was a nurse among the people. From providing health care in clinics conducted from the porch of her home, to village clinics and hospitals in the towns across Africa, Mary demonstrated God's love and healing touch to all people regardless of their religion or place in African society. She was loved by the people she served and many came to faith in Christ. One day, following Kenyan tradition, she was given a new name, Mama John, bearing the name of her son John. The name Mama John stayed with her for all the years of service across Africa and even after she returned to the States for the final assignment in Richmond, Virginia, when her husband was named regional leader for Eastern and Southern Africa in 1973.

But Mary was not happy in Richmond, so far removed from the people she loved and had lived among for so long. She began to ask God how she could still be involved in sharing His love with them. She learned the importance of prayer and committed to daily intercession for all of her co-workers and friends in the places where she had lived. But she still wanted a more closely connected ministry in person.

In 1979, she became aware of the great need for relief work in Uganda, especially the need for nurses. The nation had been devastated by a cruel regime under Idi Amin and the missionaries pleaded for help. A new missions journey was beginning that would lead to tears and heartbreak as she witnessed the ravages of war and famine that would plague Africa for years to come. For weeks and months at a time Mary served as a missionary nurse working under some of the most difficult circumstances; situations many nurses would find impossible. But Mary was creative; and the more difficult the challenge, the more she seemed to thrive, bringing smiles to the people she met.

From Uganda to Ethiopia to Somalia until well into her 70s, Mary went to feed and care for the weak, sick, and dying of Africa. She knew the power of one, the importance of each person knowing that unique place and role that God has for each of us and fulfilling it. Most of all, she committed to be all that she *could be in every circumstance of each day so the power of God could be seen and known among the people she met. She risked it all in response to Jesus' words, "I was sick and you looked after me."*

## The Story of One Missionary Hospital

*The year 2012 signals a significant anniversary in the life of one of the great success stories of Baptist medical missions work. I first began to hear about the ministries of Paraguay Baptist Medical Center years ago when I attended meetings of a Baptist medical fellowship group. One of the missionary physicians always asked me, "When are you going to Paraguay to see what God is doing through the hospital?" Sitting in my office late one night I was able to connect all the pieces of the stories I had heard through the years with the reality of where they are today. One of its former leaders and probably its strongest American advocate, Marlin Harris, came for a visit and shared the rest of their story so I might understand the continuing importance of medical missions work around the world. This hospital stands as a beacon of hope and faith in a country where 60 years ago its mission was rejected and even feared by some.*

*Miriam Willis, a missionary nurse, started a small clinic and feeding station in an area of Asunción called Chacarita. She recognized that in Paraguayan society in the 1940s one critical element of its population, the poor, lacked adequate health care. By raising awareness of this issue, a ministry was born that would eventually touch lives across the whole spectrum of Paraguay's society. Dr. Franklin and Dorcas Fowler were appointed to oversee the construction of a mission hospital in 1947 on the outskirts of Asunción, where 90 percent of the poor lived.*

*Bureaucracies and religious and professional jealousies were just a few of the barriers they faced in the early years. But the dream continued* and more missionaries arrived in 1950 to help complete the work. Within a few years the Baptist hospital opened its doors. The ministry was based on a commitment to present the gospel to every patient while building for the future and training Paraguayan nationals to one day take charge. It was a goal that would require the development of a nursing school and physician residency program with Paraguayan nationals if they were to be successful.

From the beginning, people in the poorest neighborhoods and outlying areas were told that the Baptist hospital would treat anyone who entered its doors, regardless of their ability to pay. That was not true in the government-run hospitals, so it didn't take long for word to spread. Mobile medical clinics sent into the interior to treat those who could not come to the hospital presented many opportunities to share Christ, and as a result churches sprang up. The story of how Jesus loves all people was validated by the physical care they witnessed from the missionaries.

Over the next three decades the Baptist hospital was tried and tested in many ways, but the ministry continued to provide health care for its original audience, the poor. It was something only God could do since all that was needed to sustain the hospital was supplied at just the right time. In 1987, after a major renovation of its facilities, missionaries Marlin and Jean Harris arrived in Paraguay. Their assignment: prepare the Baptist hospital for self-sufficiency under Paraguayan leadership. Three years later a five-year trial period began with Latin American Ernesto Simari serving as the hospital's assistant director. It was an unusual collaborative effort between the Baptist mission in Paraguay and representatives from the mission board alongside the Baptist Medical Center in Jacksonville, Florida. This effort resulted in a hospital business model that ensured a strong future and a great friendship between the two sharing leadership.

In 1994, the Baptist hospital leaped to a new level of care with the launch of a heart institute. Within two years, Paraguay had its first successful heart transplant. The fame of Pedro Nuñez and how he surrendered his new heart to Christ helped catapult the hospital to status as a highly recognized medical facility. Kidney transplants soon followed, as did more heart transplants.

*At the same time a newly formed entity, Centro Médico Bautista (CMB) and the hospital's independent board of directors, took complete ownership of the Baptist Medical Center, a ministry born when a nurse in a poor part of the city years ago dared to raise the banner high on behalf of those often ignored.*

*By 1998, Marlin recognized his assignment was complete. Ernesto became chief executive officer for the hospital and the Harrises returned to the States. Today, the partnership continues through a 501(c)(3) tax-exempt organization created by Marlin Harris solely to assist the Paraguay medical ministry to remain financially strong. A university has been established to train more individuals for medical support and the dream of a medical school of their own is on the horizon.*

Jesus said, "I was sick and you looked after me." I hope one day to see firsthand the miracle that has taken place in Paraguay because doctors and nurses of both countries took seriously Matthew 25. They knew that what they were doing for the least among their society was the same as doing it for Christ.

*"I was in prison and you came to visit me" (Matthew 25:36).*

The missionaries entered the platform of the church to share their testimonies one by one. Couples, young and old, committing themselves to special service shared how God had led them to this point. One of my favorite roles in my job as executive director is to be present with missionaries throughout the year as they are set aside for special service as this group was experiencing. What a joy to hear how they were trusting God with all the days ahead as they ventured into new places and new ministries. When Stacey walked up to the microphone, her presence presented the impression of a humble woman with a deep joy that seemed to radiate from her face. What she said left all of us surprised and wanting to know more of her story, a prisoner returning to prison but this time to minister.

## Stacey's Story in Her Own Words

*My name is Stacey Smith. I have two children. Matthew is 20 years old, and Desireé is 18 years old. I live in Patterson, Arkansas, where I am now working with the Lord in a ministry He is birthing, called From Prison to Purpose (P2P).*

*Growing up, I had a very normal life. I was what the world would call an all-American kid. For years, my life consisted of competing in twirling a baton and playing tennis. My mom and I traveled for years in the competition arena. These were wonderful mother-daughter years that one day we would draw from when my life would begin to take a wrong turn. As a family, we had good values; however, we did not have Christ in our lives. I was sprinkled Catholic, baptized Baptist, confirmed Episcopal, married Methodist, and then found myself in Alcoholics Anonymous with my higher power being a lightbulb. I can remember always searching but never finding.*

*At the age of 16 I began to get interested in wrong friends, which led me to wrong ways and rebellion against my parents' wishes. Shortly after this I got pregnant; and where abortion was always wrong in my family, it now began to be right because it was their daughter.*

*The first abortion led to four more. Abortion was birth control to me. My thinking was so upside down. Several suicide attempts, drug rehabs led to many more options that never seemed to help. Bad decisions led me to* many more wrong decisions, until I found myself at the age of 29 facing a 40-year to life sentence on a first-time offense drug charge. Actually, it was the first time caught versus first-time offender. My drug habit had exceeded a $400 to $500 a day habit. Immorality was a way of life for me.

I was sentenced to 60 years on this charge, which I would spend in the Arkansas Department of Corrections. During the year in county jail, there were many volunteers that shared Christ with me. But it wasn't until the week after my sentence was given that I surrendered to Christ, for Him to be the Lord of my life—whether in prison or out. I had such a deep sense of need to be forgiven. And He answered me.

I then began to pray that God would use me for the next 60 years in prison. I expressed to Him that wherever He was working in prison I desired to be a part of it. I found myself immediately having a love for His Word and a desire to live it out. Today that love for His Word and desire to live for Him has only grown stronger since that day, October 24, 1993, when I was born again. I learned after entering into the Arkansas Department of Corrections that I was not going to have to fulfill all 60 years inside the prison, but I would have to fulfill 15 of those years. I still cried out to Him to use me.

During the next 12 years of incarceration, I worked in the Chaplaincy Department, which I felt I was born to do. My beginning years in prison I was exposed to God's ways; from 1998 to release (February 2005) I was trained in God's ways through a faith-based program that God allowed me to work in with the present chaplain at the McPherson women's unit. This program taught me the "how-to" of the Christian life. These years were phenomenal, learning my position in Christ, and for that I am so grateful to my Lord. Today I think back to what I was taught in those years.

I was not supposed to be released any earlier than November 2008, at which time I would be handed over to fulfill an 11-month forgery charge in the federal system. Therefore, my earliest date of release should have been November 2009. However, God turned the heart of the governor of

*Arkansas, and he granted me clemency, which is an early-out. I left the Arkansas Department of Corrections in March 2004 and then was transported to complete my 11-month sentence with the feds. That last year the Lord taught me much and I found myself applying everything that I had learned.*

*Approximately 2 to 3 years before being released from the Arkansas Department of Corrections, the Lord began to birth a vision in my heart to help the ladies coming out of this program and being released in society. It was my desire to help them live out the truths they had learned. It was, and still is, my desire to take that one who has been bound spiritually, emotionally, and physically within the confinement of prison and help them walk in society as who they are in Christ.*

Jesus said, "I was in prison and you came to visit me." The individuals who visited Stacey and shared their faith were following the example Jesus set for the disciples. Because of their influence her life was dramatically changed, and today her testimony and witness is changing the lives of others. Through a ministry called Prison to Purpose (P2P), Stacey is reaching out to other women in prison and upon their release helping them find their place in society in healthy ways. The love and forgiveness of God radiates from her face and through her words as she shares her story with them. They know she understands more than anyone else what life has been like in prison and the darkness they face each day. But she is a symbol of hope—hope that there is One who can turn that darkness into light and give new life. Stacey not only found healing for herself but is experiencing His power in the restoring of her family as well. The journey is not over. It's not always been easy but the One who brings healing is always faithful.

# The Haven of Rest Ministry

*One of the often-overlooked tragedies of someone being sentenced to a long jail term is the devastation wreaked on families. Mothers, fathers, sisters, brothers, in addition to children and spouses of the person convicted are lives altered forever. Some allow resentment and anger to fester and shape their future in negative ways. Others see the need for personal healing and allow it to shape their thinking and become a launching pad for good. And on occasion, awareness that others share the same pain and through telling their story—a ministry is born.*

*Haven of Rest is just that, a ministry born out of shared pain and agony over the poor choices of a family member. Located just a mile from the federal prison in eastern Kentucky, it is an oasis in the sea of despair for families of individuals incarcerated; a place where loved ones traveling long distances for visitation can find respite through shared food and free lodging with people who really understand their pain.*

*In 1996, Eileen Mullins, the founder of Haven of Rest, learned firsthand what this kind of tragedy does to a family. One of her sons at age 32 was sentenced to 20 years in prison after killing his wife in a divorce dispute. This experience could have totally devastated her life and that of her family. As a retired teacher and minister's wife, her life had been about helping others, not dealing with this kind of situation personally. Rather than allow this tragedy to end her life, she turned to the one thing that was constant— her faith. She prayed for strength and that her situation might be turned into good. She trusted God to lead her as she took one step at a time into the future. Visiting her son, she and her husband soon recognized their shared plight with other families with one exception—many did not have a faith foundation from which to draw strength. With no available gathering space for families to talk to each other, she began to ask God how she* could help. The day she learned a federal prison would be built near her hometown she knew God's purpose for her future.

After much prayer and planning, sharing her vision with anyone that would listen, Haven of Rest was born in 2004. Manned by volunteers and funded through donations, the ministry has touched the lives of untold numbers of families of prison inmates.

The facility was built on four acres of donated land by volunteers who caught a vision of what God could do. Today, Haven of Rest offers a place where families can find nourishment not only for their physical bodies but for their souls. Its success is a result of the faithfulness of founder Eileen Mullins, who remained true to His purposes, claiming His promise from Romans 8:28: "In all things God works for the good of those who love him, who have been called according to his purpose."

Peter and John faced prison more than once in their lifetime. Others who proclaimed the truths of Jesus' claims were also persecuted. They endured because they knew the stories of Jesus were true. Their lives had been radically changed by the power of the gospel and the presence of the Holy Spirit. They also were blessed by those who ministered to them when they found themselves in prison.

Paul wrote in several of his letters about his gratitude for the ministry he had received. In Philippians 1:3 he shared: "I thank my God every time I remember you. In all my prayers for all of you, I always pray with joy because of your partnership in the gospel from the first day until now." As we experience the challenges of life in our own personal ways, the understanding and kindness of strangers and family, friends and acquaintances often brings much joy and peace.

# Reflections

How are you connected to the story of faith?
Have you traced a lineage of faith from previous generations
in your family to the present? Have you received the love and
compassion from others who are connected to faith in Christ?
Or maybe you are one who has been called to ministry and found
that unique way to express your love for Christ to others. As we
minister to "the least of these" or if we are one of the least, let's
make sure we connect the ministry with the story, for the presence
of Christ is the only true source of strength and hope
for our lives.

Section 3

Commit

Chapter 7

Stories Begin
with One Voice

*H*istory is filled with stories of individuals and small groups who have had a major influence on society. In a previous chapter I highlighted the impact of John Newton and William Wilberforce on slavery in England. With every issue of an insult against human dignity there has arisen a voice, then a few voices, and finally a chorus of voices until the message was heard and change took place. But it usually began with one.

The beginnings of the Christian church were born from small numbers. Jesus spoke out in a prophetic voice and called the 12, then 70, then 120 in the upper room. With the power of God at work, the story of Jesus exploded against all odds, spreading beyond Jerusalem to Judea, Samaria, and eventually the rest of the world, and spanning the centuries. Underneath it all was a personal commitment to tell the story of Jesus no matter the obstacle or challenge.

The word *commitment* is not always a popular one today. For example, in the United States where I live, we boast of our individual rights, of how critical it is to be my own person and do things my own way. With a divorce rate of 50 percent or more, both within and outside the church, evidence speaks for itself of our lack of understanding when it comes to the meaning of commitment. But within the faith community, commitment to Christ and to a cause beyond ourselves can be found.

*WMU, a ministry that will celebrate 125 years of service in 2013, began as the result of a small group of women who heard God's call to be missions*

advocates during a day when women had little voice. They were not allowed to vote in public elections and had few choices for creating their own financial resources. Missionaries were pleading for the people to come and serve, but few churches were listening. One voice, then more voices, often in isolated areas, found each other and grew to a small group. They were women of great faith who had caught a vision of how much God loved all the people of the world, not just people like themselves. They dreamed of a great movement for mission support and began to speak out even when it wasn't acceptable. They modeled how to use meager resources to help the poor and lift up the disadvantaged.

As their organization grew, they spoke out on slavery, racism, AIDS, whatever the issue in their generation that created barriers to telling and receiving the story of Jesus. It took commitment as individual women and as an organization to know and faithfully follow God's call to missions. This part of our history still shapes our future today. But it all began with the personal commitment of a few brave women.

I began my WMU journey as a young pastor's wife learning the ropes of church life and discovering where I might use my gifts in service. My first job in the church was leading a group of teenage girls called Acteens® in missions education. It was the beginning of God's work in my life to open my eyes and heart to a world I knew very little about. One of the great things about being a part of WMU is the opportunity for leadership development. I quickly recognized (and I suspect others did as well) that my nursing skills did not qualify me to teach teenagers. I needed help and WMU provided it. As a side benefit to attending summer training sessions, there was always a missionary speaker. It was a gradual awareness at first, but slowly the message sank in that God doesn't use just preachers and missionaries in His work. He uses ordinary people like me and yes, even teenage girls. We were learning together and the more we ventured out into our community on missions projects, the more we learned.

After our family served in St. Vincent, we returned home and Larry was called to pastor a church in Georgia. One of my first jobs in the church, again, was to work with teenage girls in Acteens. It became my entry point into state WMU work. I met wonderful leaders who spent much of their time equipping laypeople like me in the work of missions education. Summers as a volunteer nurse at the children's missions camp, teaching others how to lead Acteens (now that I was the experienced one) all deepened my leadership skills in the work of the church and missions. My heart for personal missions involvement continued as I traveled with medical missions teams back to St. Vincent and then to Brazil.

In 1993, I was asked to serve as president for the state organization of WMU in Georgia. I don't think anyone was more surprised than me when this opportunity presented itself. There were others who were older and wiser, I thought, but it became clear God was calling me to something new. I loved my nursing profession and I loved WMU. I soon discovered that God was providing further leadership development experiences and opportunities to serve in ways I had never imagined. The president in a state organization automatically has a place on the national board of WMU. What a privilege to meet others from across the United States who shared my passion for missions and WMU. I soaked up all that God was teaching me through the leaders I met and the training I experienced at national events. I loved getting to know the women in churches all across my state who were committed to Christ and His mission and lived it week in and week out through their church and in the places of ministry that God had called them.

Then in a very surprising meeting of fellow state presidents in 1996, I was asked to serve as the national president. All of my past experiences, my commitment to missions education and involvement, my belief that God, for His glory, wanted to use WMU—an organization that had grown from very small beginnings to being almost a million strong— seemed to come together. I sensed God was bringing all of these, along with my professional career in nursing, into a significant moment in my journey. My story, one that seemed so small and insignificant, was being enriched in ways I could never have imagined. I found my abilities as a leader stretched and my dependence on God for strength and wisdom greater than ever before.

In 2000, life took a rather strange turn for me and my family. Dellanna O'Brien, WMU executive director for 10 years, had retired following a stroke and WMU was seeking the next executive director. As the search committee prayed and sought God's direction, they spoke with me several times. I will never forget my husband challenging me to seek God's will in this situation and not close my heart to a change if He in fact was leading me to consider the position. After much prayer and soul-searching, I sensed God's call yet again to something I felt woefully ill-equipped to handle. I remember asking myself on many occasions during that first year as executive director, How on earth did I get here? And then I remembered. Just as God had called me to missions long ago, He was calling me to this new role and He would sustain me each day as I placed my faith and trust in Him alone.

During the past decade, I have learned much about the call to leadership, especially in the day-to-day challenges of ministry and leading a nonprofit organization that publishes resources for churches and individuals that want to have a radical impact for Christ. When I have needed new skills, I found willing teachers. When I needed wisdom, I found experts willing to share with me. But above all, God has been present in every situation.

During my second year, the attack on the World Trade Center took place and the security of financial reserves to sustain our work was suddenly gone. Denominational conflict took its toll the next few years as we sought to reach new churches with our resources and stabilize the business side of our ministry. Reaching out to other professionals in the field of finance and nonprofit work, as well as more seasoned *denominational leaders, proved helpful as I worked my way through each issue. But all of the best advice and leadership training cannot lead to success unless the Lord has called you to the task and you allow Him to work in the midst of the day-to-day as well as in your personal life. It requires a commitment of one's total self to the calling of God if you are to succeed.*

*I have been blessed to work with some of the greatest people both in our offices in Birmingham and in our states with WMU partners. I've witnessed their commitment and strong belief that missions is a vital part of growing as a Christian. Their dedication has always encouraged me to press on as their leader. I've made my share of mistakes and received much grace along the way. I hope I have given half as much to others as they have given to me on this journey. But one thing I know for certain. For any ministry, organization, business, or church to survive the kind of testing both culturally and economically as we have faced in the past 10 years, you must know your purpose and feel confident that God is walking with you as you fulfill that purpose. Otherwise you will fail.*

*The beauty of WMU throughout its history is that it has always known its purpose—missions. We have been accused from time to time of trying to be all things to all people, but we have always come back to our core message. Missions has been defined as what God does through the church to extend the gospel in both word and deed to all the people of the world. Our part, our calling, is to challenge people and churches to allow Him to work through them to engage those who need to know His story and provide the opportunities for people to be involved in telling His story. It's an amazing gift from God to be a part of His work for so many years. The singular thread since 1888 has been the commitment of one woman to lead another and then another to understand and embrace God's call for their day.*

# Defining Commitment

I read an interesting definition on a Web-based dictionary that says *commitment* means "the act of binding yourself to a course of action." It is feeling loyalty to something and implies dependability on a person's word. Growing up, my children often heard a warning that if they started something, I expected them to finish it. I saw some of their classmates begin a project and drop out before it was completed, or join a club or music group only to decide they didn't want to stay with it to the end of the term. Each time someone did not follow through it left a hole which others had to fill. I knew commitment was something to be taught. Part of their maturing into adulthood where they could be counted on to keep commitments would require learning these lessons early. But it was not without its challenges at times.

*For instance, when Matt wanted to take piano lessons like his sister, we discussed how much practice it would require and that he would have to go to weekly lessons. Not long after he started he learned just how hard it was to practice and master all that the teacher expected. He wanted to quit but he stuck with it for the agreed-upon time because he made a commitment.*

*The same was true with sports. When he wanted to play soccer, I worried about his physical ability to do so. He had serious problems with asthma and there would be times it would be a real challenge for him. At the same time, if he committed to play, I wanted him to know the team would be counting on him to finish the year. We were fortunate to have an understanding coach who believed as I did that once he started, we had to help him finish well. The coach worked out a plan that fit the situation.*

*Matt would play a quarter and then a substitute would play. He would play the next quarter and then sit out again. It was the perfect solution. He stuck with the team as long as his age allowed him to participate in this particular soccer program. He learned a lot about commitment as he pressed through some of the physical challenges of the game. His understanding of finishing what you start has served him well through college, graduate studies, and today as a pediatric health-care professional, all of which presented opportunities to walk away when the going got tough. But he was committed to see it through and because of his faith, knew God would walk with him to completion.*

*Allison followed the same understanding as Matt that once she started something, she had to finish. One of the more difficult times would come in college when she started down a path of piano performance. She had begun playing the piano before her feet could touch the pedals. She loved music and tried multiple instruments through school and community orchestras but piano was always her favorite. After 14 years of piano lessons, she entered college with a degree in mind. I will never forget the phone call after one of the performance exams required at the end of a semester her sophomore year. Sobbing, she said she just couldn't continue. At first I thought she would push through, but when she said the pressure to perform was taking away her love for music, I knew we had given this commitment requirement all we could. I'm the first to admit there are times when you step back and reevaluate the circumstances, and when enough effort has been exerted it could be God has a different plan and is releasing you.*

*Today she loves music, loves the piano, has been the church pianist for several churches, and has a beautiful baby grand sitting in her living room. She is conscious of the importance of music in a child's life and exposes her children whenever possible, teaching them to love music as well. But God was indeed intervening in her path, which led her to law school and to advocacy work among some of the poor and disadvantaged of our state. As an advocate for building a stronger community network to intervene in families experiencing domestic violence, she teaches youth about the value of life and how to treat one another with respect. She trains police in how to respond to domestic calls and works with the court system for fair and responsible treatment as well as punishment for the offender. She made a commitment to take her faith with her into the workplace and one step at a time, one person at a time, she is making a difference. As is always the case, there have been moments when she wanted to quit. Life can be ugly and hard when dealing with this kind of tragedy in families but she sticks with it. She is quick to say God has called her as she presses on.*

What is your view of commitment? What experiences have you encountered where someone failed to keep a commitment to you or some project in which you were involved? What impact have you had on the life of another when you failed to keep your own commitment or when you stuck with something that was so difficult you thought you just couldn't keep on? Our story is built on the foundation of commitment of others to share the story of Jesus. While our life journey will find different expressions for our faith, the commitment to keep the story alive for generations to come is vitally important.

The Apostle Paul reminds us of his understanding of faith commitment. Life had become very difficult as he stood for his faith and defended the power of the gospel to work in his day when he spoke these words: *Forgetting what is behind and straining toward what is ahead, I press on toward the goal to win the prize for which God has called me heavenward in Christ Jesus (Philippians 3:13–14).*

Powerful words from a man who was once so committed to stopping the story of Jesus from being told. But once he met the

Jesus of the story, Paul's life direction changed dramatically and he was committed until the end of his life.

I've lived most of my adult life within the framework of the church and denomination. I love the church, love being a part of the programs of the church, and love the fellowship with believers in the church. I have learned, matured, and developed as a Christian because of the church. There is an important role for the church in proclaiming the gospel and shaping society as well as individuals. Peter's declaration about the church in his first epistle says it clearly. "But you are a chosen people, a royal priesthood, a holy nation, a people belonging to God, that you may declare the praises of him who called you out of darkness into his wonderful light" (1 Peter 2:9).

The world needs to see ordinary people living out their faith commitment each day if the story of Jesus is to live on impacting the present as well as the next generation. Peter went on to say in that same passage, "Live such good lives among the pagans that, though they accuse you of doing wrong, they may see your good deeds and glorify God on the day he visits us" (v. 12). He is echoing what he learned from Jesus who said, "In the same way, let your light shine before men, that they may see your good deeds and praise your Father in heaven" (Matthew 5:16).

It saddens me to read various surveys in recent years that indicate fewer and fewer people are finding faith through the activities of the church. At the same time, I'm encouraged when I realize the more powerful message that is being preached through the believer who lives it out each day in the workplace and at home, in his community, at ball games and school activities, even as he or she drinks coffee at a coffee shop engaging people in conversation. Faith commitment is the most important commitment we make and has an everlasting effect on those who know us and are seeking a better way. Most often the story of Jesus and His impact on our lives becomes a living story others can see and begin to ask their own faith questions. As a person of faith who loves the church, I am committed to connecting the two, the personal lifestyle of a follower of Christ that is also integrated into the life of the church. Jesus came and died so the church universal might live on to bring all people into a relationship with Him. The two must be connected for the story to live on in a way that changes lives for eternity.

## Story of Angola Prison and Burl Cain

*Burl Cain is an amazing man. He understands that the Christian faith involves more than a compartmentalized view of life, that a person's faith is the foundation for who we are in every aspect of life as we interact with people on a daily basis. He brought that belief system to his role as warden in what has often been referred to as the "bloodiest prison in the country."*

*Started in 1901, the Louisiana State Penitentiary, better known as Angola, is located 59 miles northwest of Baton Rouge. With more than 5,000 inmates, 1,800 employees, and a budget of approximately $84 million, Angola exists as a town unto itself on 1,800 acres that were once a plantation. All physically able inmates are required to work in the prison's farming operations. Eight hours a day, five days a week they plant, tend, and harvest crops that include corn, soybeans, tomatoes, cabbage, okra, watermelons, and more. They tend to an estimated 1,500 cattle in addition to the food crops. Others work in programs that create license tags, mops and brooms, metal fabrication, and silk screening. This is and will be the life for most of the inmates at Angola since more than half are serving life sentences. The next highest groups are serving an average of 49.75 years,* *making it practically a life sentence depending on their age at confinement. Violent criminals make up 87 percent of the population.*

*When Burl Cain entered as warden in 1995, there were 799 reported attacks on inmates and 192 on guards. Murder, suicide, attacks on one another all seemed to stem from a sense of hopelessness prevalent throughout the prison. Burl felt he had to change the culture, restore a sense of hope among the hopeless, and alter the dynamics of prison life. Without a model for how to do this, he began with educational opportunities through arts and crafts clubs and a Dale Carnegie self-improvement course, hoping these would help inmates develop new skills and interests.*

*As a man of faith, he believed a moral rehabilitation had to begin as well. He reached out to New Orleans Baptist Theological Seminary for help. An undergraduate college degree program was begun; instead of working the fields students who qualified could enroll and take classes. In 2010, 150 inmates had earned a bachelor of arts degree and an additional 100 were on track to finish their degree. Course work is the same for prison inmates as it is for those in a regular college setting, so a deep desire for an education on the part of the individual was needed. As they interact with the professors from New Orleans Seminary, a fresh perspective on their future and their faith is possible.*

*But the real story lies in the men who have graduated with a seminary degree and are now serving their fellow inmates. As they heard the stories of Jesus and were challenged to give their hearts to Christ through the church services in the prison, men began to receive salvation and hear God's call to ministry. But with years left on their sentences, following that call into ministry seemed impossible; that is, until they realized God could use them right where they were. One inmate, Jerome Derricks, said he had run from God's call "all my life. But I like to put it like this: God finds people wherever they go." Today he serves as the pastor of the prison church in the reception center where new prisoners begin their time, as well as ministering to almost 100 men on death row.*

*Burl understands the importance of connecting people from all walks of life with the story of Jesus. And as the men grew in their faith, a natural desire for sharing their faith emerged. Prisoners reaching prisoners for Christ is a compelling model of service. Who better to help explain the issues of life in this setting than someone who lives in their same situation every day? Paul Will, a prisoner from New Jersey serving a life sentence, said, "We made mistakes and we ended up here, but our lives haven't ended. We can still do some good in this world."*

*Today, in more than 18 churches and counseling centers within the prison, these men are serving as pastors and counselors ministering to the physical and emotional hurts of the men as well as leading to faith those who will listen. A transformation is slowly taking place at Angola; and as it began, other prison wardens were curious. They wanted to know what their fellow warden was doing that was making such a difference. The more they learned, the more they wanted the same model for their prisons. But how could they make it work? It would take someone who had been through the program to make it happen in another setting if it were to really be effective. The idea was discussed among the inmates at Angola; and when the opportunity was presented, 23 New Orleans graduates accepted the call to become missionaries in eight satellite prisons across Louisiana. The model has now spread beyond Louisiana into Mississippi and Georgia prisons with others on the horizon.*

*A miracle is taking place in Angola. God is at work in the lives of prisoners and prison staff, among New Orleans professors and families, as they see some of the most hardened criminals turn to Christ for complete healing. It all began when one man realized his commitment to Christ was not just on Sundays at church but in every aspect of his life, including his role as warden at Angola.*

## Reflections

*Commitment*, "the act of binding yourself to a course of action." Long after Peter and John responded to Jesus' invitation to "come, follow me" (Matthew 4:19), they were faced with challenges and obstacles to staying the course. With every test of faith came assurance from Jesus who said, "'I am the way and the truth and the life. No one comes to the Father except through me'" (John 14:6). Their commitment to Jesus and the way of salvation He presented began as a small voice that grew to a chorus and spread across the world. They were bound to a course of action and because of their commitment the story lives on today.

Where does your commitment lie? Is it tied to the truth of Jesus and His words? As you think about your everyday life, are you living in such a way that others can see Him and desire to follow? Commitment is a costly thing, but when it is a commitment to Jesus nothing else matters.

Chapter 8 Stories of Unsung Heroes

*A* commitment to follow Jesus includes learning how to give the gift of ourselves to others. The Bible is full of stories of individuals who gave far above and beyond what was expected in their religious culture. Jesus presented an even more radical approach to giving in the stories He told. One of those is found in the Gospel of Mark where Jesus taught a very important lesson for the disciples on the true spirit of giving. He was observing the crowd putting money in the offering receptacle that day. Rich people had put in large amounts and then He observed a widow, someone with few resources, who

*came and put in two very small copper coins, worth only a fraction of a penny. Calling the disciples to him, Jesus said, "I tell you the truth, this poor widow has put more into the treasury than all the others. They gave out of their wealth; but she, out of her poverty, put in everything—all she had to live on" (Mark 12:42–44).*

I realize this passage is usually one we attribute to stewardship lessons, particularly on the giving of our money. But I think the significance goes deeper than just money. I think Jesus would remind us it is the spirit in which we give of ourselves. Our attitude about how we spend our money is often a reflection on those things that are most important to us. For the person we love deeply, we probably find it easier to spend our money than when it is someone we don't know or maybe someone we don't like. The same is true in giving of our time. It is one of the most precious commodities we have today. We want time to do those things we like to do, to work at the things we feel called to, and often feel put upon when our time is used doing something we don't think is important. It is a part of our me-first culture to want to focus on what we like rather than what might be needed by others.

In this passage Jesus reminds us that when we give out of a spirit of thanksgiving and love, even if our gift seems insignificant compared to those who can give much, it's not only acceptable, but maybe even preferred in God's eyes. It's not always the big things we do that last; often the small gifts of time, the gift of our presence offered out of a heart of love make the most difference.

*It had been a long day of celebrating his brother's birthday. Bennett, our four-year-old grandson, had done so well watching him open lots of presents and enjoy a party with all his friends. But as the night wore on so did his usual gentle spirit and patience. A squabble erupted, there were tears, and then hugs with reminders he would have a birthday one day too. Without any prodding from parents, Russell came to Bennett and gave him one of his birthday presents, something he already had and was going to return to the store for a trade. He didn't make a big deal out of it, just handed it to him and walked off. Without a moment's hesitation Bennett jumped up, ran after him, and threw his arms around him from behind. And with as much love as he knew to express, said, "You're the best brother in the whole world." Watching this play out was one of those special gifts for a grandparent. My eyes met my daughter's and without saying a word we knew this was a rare moment.*

Teaching young children to love others, to share their toys, to say please and thank you are not always the easiest tasks. But it is an important part of building a foundation for faith that is yet to come. When you pair this with quality lessons from the Bible at church and home, the chances of the meaning of real love, agape love, sticking is more likely. Week in and week out unsung heroes and heroines of the faith show up on Sundays, Wednesday nights, at morning programs for moms, and other times to teach children about God. This is their calling and their gift of themselves as Jesus taught.

*One of the most important ministries in the churches of which I have been a member, when it comes to shaping the hearts and minds of young girls, is called Girls in Action® (GA®). Begun in 1913 out of a desire to help prepare future generations of young women to hear and respond to God's call, GA has become a continuous thread of influence for more than 100 years. So many female missionaries and church leaders when sharing their testimonies will say, "When I was a GA I learned . . ."*

*One day at a gathering of WMU leaders someone started to repeat what was called the Star Ideals, a pledge from years ago memorized by young girls as they participated in GA. In that brief moment a chorus of voices rose spontaneously from the group as they began quoting with a growing sense of excitement this important learning moment from their past. When they finished, a cheer and applause erupted, and I think for many a private renewal of commitments made long ago surfaced, to pass on that experience to the next generation.*

*Chapter 8*

# The Stories of Unsung Heroes

*Robin Hoke is one of those who benefited from early influences in church. A wife, mother, and art teacher from Midland, Texas, Robin grew up with her mother and grandmother modeling the importance of teaching others in missions. For many years both women were devoted leaders in missions education through WMU. Robin says she was blessed to have her mother as her GA director and creator of GA coronations, an event which affirmed the work of young girls in missions. These experiences, shared by mother and daughter, became some of her best childhood memories.*

*Looking back on those times she said, "My years in missions education as a GA helped me to know God, understand His plan for the world, and discover my place in His plan. What [children] learn in missions education opens their eyes to see, their hearts to care, and their hands to serve. Discipleship through missions education affects you eternally; which is why I say, once a GA, always a GA."*

*Several years ago Robin received a national award for her outstanding service as a leader of GA spanning more than 22 years. When she accepted the award she commented, "If receiving this award gives me the platform to speak to people and explain the value of teaching missions to children, then I am thrilled. If we expect future generations to live out the Great Commission as adults, we must begin to teach them the concept when they are young. That is my heart, my calling, my passion for service."*

*As a young military wife in the mid-1950s, Sara Clayton began to teach preschoolers and young girls about Jesus and how they were to be involved in telling His stories to their friends. She knew how important it was to help lay a foundation for faith early with children because of her own experiences as a child. She became involved in missions through her church*

*during the early 1940s when she attended GA. She soaked up what she was learning and one year even sold hamburgers to raise money to attend GA camp where she could learn more.*

*After marriage, wherever her husband was stationed, Sara found ways to be involved and to involve others in missions through a local church. From leading summer Bible clubs to organizing youth and adult missions trips to hosting international students and missionaries in their home, Sara continued to model the impact of missions learning in a person's everyday life. After suffering a stroke in her later years, unable to speak, Sara didn't give up. In her quiet, unassuming way she found other avenues where she could serve, meeting the needs before her. Sara would tell you she has never done anything particularly unusual in her life, but many would disagree. I think her daughter, Joyce, said it best. "My mother does not understand she has been extraordinary because she thinks it's ordinary to be involved."*

*Like Sara, Joy Cranford developed a love for missions as a young girl in GA and has lived a life committed to sharing the love of Christ ever since. When asked about Joy, those who know her best responded in some specific ways.*

*One said, "Joy learned as a GA that 'We've a Story to Tell' and she has made telling that story her life work." Another commented, "Joy lives out her love for Christ by sharing God's love and compassion every day, and she challenges others to be on mission as she leads girls and women."*

*In addition to her leadership in the local church, Joy has participated in several missions trips to China, taught English as a second language, and volunteered locally since 1996 in Christian Women's Job Corps® (CWJC®), a Christian-based job skills readiness ministry begun by WMU. Taking what she learned as a child and allowing that knowledge to shape who she became as an adult, someone that gives back so others can hear, is what faith is all about.*

Other important but often unsung heroes in our churches are the nursery workers, those who prepare the meals for fellowship times, and many others who simply find their place in service. They use their gifts and express their love for Jesus by giving quietly and in unassuming ways week after week in the work of the church. What they do provides support so others can hear the stories of Jesus and find their place in service.

For some, teaching children is not their gift. They have skills and talents that are best used in ministries that help extend the church's witness to the community. Some find volunteering at the rescue mission, feeding the homeless, visiting the sick in the hospital, or taking a meal when they are home is their gift. They are always the first ones to organize the project and see that it happens. Their work likewise often goes unnoticed by most and with few words of thanks from the ones who are helped. But they do it because God has called them, not for the thank-you.

*Susan lost her job and thought her life was over. To fill her days she began to volunteer at a local ministry center where churches provided clothes and food for families experiencing hardships. When she heard they needed help in the afternoons, she began to go over after school to assist with tutoring and to listen as the students voiced their problems. Before long she realized God was calling her to this ministry. She asked me one day if I thought she could be appointed as a missionary. She had been divorced and did not have the education usually required, but I told her she*

*The Story Lives On*

*should try anyway. When she didn't qualify for a paid position, she accepted the designation of a Mission Service Corps volunteer and raised her own support because the calling was so clear. The last time I saw Susan she was an outstanding leader among the churches in her town, calling out others to give of themselves in service to those in need. She not only tells the stories of Jesus to the families that pass through the doors of the center but she models Jesus every day in the way she loves and gives of herself.*

## Christian Women's Job Corps and Christian Men's Job Corps

Across our nation in more than 300 sites teachers, judges, accountants, nurses, and others with a variety of backgrounds and skills are pooling their resources to help men and women who need a second chance at life. Under various titles that fit their location, the framework of Christian Women's Job Corps (CWJC) and Christian Men's Job Corps® (CMJC^SM) exists to provide assistance for some who have just come out of prison, others who have lost financial support through death or divorce, and those who have only known the cycle of poverty for most of their lives.

*Following a missions tour in the Appalachian region of the United States, a host of WMU state leaders met to discuss what they had experienced. The images of poverty, hunger, joblessness, and more struck to the heart of each person on the trip. My predecessor at WMU, Dellanna O'Brien, told of meeting a woman with probably less than a third-grade education who had established a ministry center in one of the mountain communities. Somehow she was providing food and clothing to many in her area with the*

most meager resources of her own. Dellanna was so struck by the tenacity and commitment of this woman she said in her heart she knew she and WMU had to do something to help.

Months later, after laying the foundation for study and research, a seed of an idea was born and plans for four pilot projects emerged in four states. It was important to identify the common characteristics for a ministry that could be sustained and managed by the average layperson in any community who saw the need and knew this was God's calling. In 1997, after a successful series of pilots and evaluations, Christian Women's Job Corps began as a way of equipping people with life and employment skills experienced in a Christian context. Thousands of women since that time have found faith through the Bible studies, employment through job readiness skills, stronger self-esteem, and self-confidence that so many lacked when they came into the program.

**Shadale Hodges was one of those who came out of a background of drugs, alcohol, and domestic violence. Her finances were in total disarray when she entered the program and life seemed hopeless. In 2008, she heard about CWJC and enrolled. An unexpected gift came when she met Pat Bryan, her mentor, a Christian woman who would commit to meet with her regularly and be the cheerleader she so desperately needed. The first step was to set her family on a budget and help her find ways to support them during this transition. Shadale recently stated that Mrs. Pat (as she refers to her) "became a part of my family and provided my children and me with a new outlook on life."**

**In addition to financial planning and job readiness training, Shadale attended the CWJC Bible studies and began to grow in her faith, understanding that God desired a better way of life for her and**

*her children. Today Shadale is seeking a college education in hopes of becoming a drug abuse counselor. She said, "I want to use my knowledge and experience to help others who may be struggling as well. I want to be able to reach out and encourage others who may be hopeless, letting them know that there is hope." Pat Bryan and hundreds of others like her are influencing the Shadales of this world because they realize their faith is not just words, not just attending church, but investing themselves in the lives of hurting of people in their communities. But it doesn't come easily. It requires a commitment of the heart and the will to stick with it when the success story doesn't come quickly. Change doesn't happen overnight when people have few positive influences in their lives; but it does happen, and when it comes, what a visible sign of God at work in both lives.*

Small groups of men who were aware of the women's program began to take notice of its success. They realized that many of the same approaches used for women would work with men in similar circumstances.

*A small group in San Angelo, Texas, performed their own pilot and measured their results. I was sitting with this group of Christian men in a meeting at our offices when they asked if they could become a part of WMU. In that moment, in 2004, Christian Men's Job Corps was born.*

*Many individuals coming through the men's program are coming from prison. One of the participants who shared his testimony said he had been in prison most of his life and knew there had to be a better way when he got out. He wanted to change and came looking for help. Fortunately, CMJC was ready and willing and his life is dramatically different today. The gift of time and listening, of compassion and grace found in GA leaders and CWJC mentors are examples of the kind of giving Jesus talked about in Mark 12. It is a gift of ourselves so His story can be told.*

## The Commitment of One Woman

*Diana Lewis, a much-loved missionary for more than 20 years in Arkansas, is one of those quiet servants that has made a lasting impact on a community that many people forget exists. In the small, impoverished area known as Dixonville, Diana began to build relationships. Her friend, Sandy Wisdom-Martin, remembers traveling down a rough, dirt road to get to a place where they would offer assistance.*

**As we rode through that community, the children came running from everywhere. One little boy jumped off his bicycle and left it on the side of the road because he could not peddle over the ruts fast enough to reach Diana. . . . I always have that image in my mind, of people running to her. What kind of relationship do you need to nurture with people that they are so excited to see you that they come running to you . . . that they can't wait to hear what you have to say about Jesus?**

The people of Dixonville know about Jesus because Diana has told them the stories, but more importantly she has shown them what it means to be one of God's servants. Her long-term commitment to be a presence in this community has demonstrated the depth of her love for Jesus as well as His children. Working in this economically challenged place could blind people to the potential for joy behind the poverty. The faces of children who love Diana are a reminder that one woman committed to following Jesus can become the face of hope as they experience faith in Him.

Sometimes when we read the stories of those who have performed outstanding service, we think what we do is not as important. We wonder if we have missed something along the way since we see ourselves as just ordinary people. The truth is, when we give of ourselves because of the love and grace we have received from Christ, our service is just as important as the extraordinary things we sometimes read about. In reality, when we are no longer living, it is often that service which others remember and celebrate.

## Charlie's Story

*Recently I attended the funeral of a very special friend. Charlie loved the Lord, his family, the church, and WMU. As a minister of education, he became a part of my husband's life when Larry was a teenager. He was a continuous presence throughout those years when Larry lost both of his parents. Charlie was also there when we met and married, when our children were born, when they graduated from high school, and when they married. Charlie was one of those rare people who never failed to call on your birthday or other important family occasions. Many who spoke at his funeral said he had a knack for just showing up at the right moment when they needed a listening ear or a caring word. He never stayed long but just long enough.*

*When my children were young, Charlie would drop in to spend the night* when he was passing through our town. He always left his signature mark —a Diet Dr Pepper—a case of which he usually carried in his trunk everywhere he went. If for some reason he didn't have one, he would leave 50 cents on their beds so they could buy one for themselves. When our daughter went off to college, she would sometimes call and say Charlie came by her dorm that day. And when we would ask about their visit, she would say, "Oh, I didn't see him. I just found the Diet Dr Pepper by my door."

On a cold January day in 2000 I was elected to serve as WMU executive director. Thinking I might be a bit nervous while the discussions among the Board members were taking place, Charlie called and asked if he could take my family to breakfast at a restaurant not too far from the WMU offices. We were enjoying good food and sharing special memories when I was notified of the Board's decision. From time to time Charlie would mention that day and smile with a twinkle in his eye. He always prayed for me, wrote letters telling me of his support, and occasionally a check would arrive in the mail with a note saying he wanted to help pay the light bill at WMU that month.

Besides the Diet Dr Pepper that was frequently with him, Charlie had a second trademark. He always wore a bow tie. I can't remember a time when I saw him wearing a regular tie. And so in honor of Charlie, on the day of his funeral many wore a bowtie to pay tribute to this sweet man with a servant's heart. It wasn't the big things about Charlie's life that we celebrated, it was the simple things he did to demonstrate love and compassion because he had experienced the same from Jesus.

In his book Twelve Ordinary Men John MacArthur wrote of the disciples: "Although they were common men, theirs was an uncommon calling." Charlie was a common man with an uncommon calling. He was known for visiting the hospital or walking around town to speak to people just because he wanted to check in on them. He prayed for people regularly; and when there was a need, he did what he could to help meet it. In his own right, he was an important disciple that people will miss. There are many others like Charlie who quietly tell the stories of Jesus by the way they love and care for people.

*Jesus said,*

*"I tell you the truth, this poor widow has put more into the treasury than all the others. They gave out of their wealth; but she, out of her poverty, put in everything—all she had to live on" (Mark 12:43–44).*

The stories of these individuals and many more like them are examples of people who have given everything they have in service to the people God placed in their paths. Their quiet, selfless spirit and commitment to demonstrating the love and compassion of Jesus is a visible story of the calling to follow Jesus into the world.

As I reflect on the individuals I have met in the churches where my husband served as pastor and the ones in which we have been members, there are many Charlies, Joys, Saras, and Dianas. Their names are different but their service given joyfully week after week teaching children, working in the ministry centers of their hometowns, and sharing the story of Jesus in their daily contacts at work is incredible. We have been called to serve a wonderful God, to follow a living Savior who understands our needs, our sorrows, and our joys. The challenge is to see all the possibilities for service and discern the path He would have us take.

# Reflections

What is He calling you to see and commit to as you serve Him? What are the obstacles that might prevent you from taking up the cause? As we tell Him our struggles, give Him the obstacles, we might be surprised when He moves them all aside and allows us the joy that follows serving Him.

Chapter 9 — The Story Includes Many Lives

*O*ne of my favorite books of the Old Testament is Nehemiah. Years ago when God was preparing me for a special assignment in a country that was far from open to the story of Jesus, I had been studying this book in personal devotions. Imagine my surprise when I discovered I would be traveling to the places mentioned throughout this book. Since that time I have gone back to reread the story of Nehemiah, gleaning new truths about leadership and about God's provision when we are faithful. Nehemiah provides a picture of what happens when a person is committed to prayer and to following God's direction in the large and small challenges of life.

*The opening chapter of the Book of Nehemiah reveals a great deal about a man who served the king as a cupbearer or close servant. He tasted all the food and drink before it made it to the king's lips. If someone tried to poison the king, guess who died first? The cupbearer. God had a special task for Nehemiah, one that would require the cooperation of many others for him to be successful.*

*One day the king asked him why he looked so sad; and when Nehemiah told him about his home, Jerusalem, being in ruins, the king asked what he could do to help. Before he ever responded, Scripture says Nehemiah prayed. He had been praying for several days once the news had come about the walls being broken and the gates burned leaving those who had returned home in a desperate situation. He sought God's direction and intervention in the situation; but when the king asked how he could help, he paused to pray once more. With the king's blessing and letters to* the governors of dangerous lands through which he would pass, he embraced the call to help his people rebuild Jerusalem.

When faced with a new challenge, many leaders believe it is important to come in strong and establish yourself as the person in charge. But not Nehemiah. The first thing he did when he arrived in Jerusalem was to gather a small group to examine the reality and heighten their awareness of the situation. Only when they saw the depth of the problem did he issue a challenge to rebuild the wall. He reminded them of his experience of God's presence with him on his journey so far. They caught his vision, believed as he did that it could be done if they worked together, and began rebuilding. Little by little others joined the effort and soon families were building whatever portion of the wall was most closely connected to where they lived. Over and over he led them to pray and offered words of encouragement. Numerous times threats from outside the city came and people were fearful, but Nehemiah continued to say, "'Don't be afraid of them. Remember the Lord, who is great and awesome, and fight for your brothers, your sons and your daughters, your wives and your homes'" (Nehemiah 4:14), and they returned to work.

**So the wall was completed on the twenty-fifth of Elul, in fifty-two days. When all our enemies heard about this, all the surrounding nations were afraid and lost their self-confidence, because they realized that this work had been done with the help of our God (Nehemiah 6:15–16).**

Nehemiah had a clear vision of God's call and the importance of the task. He persevered through all the obstacles and threats of reprisals and he prayed continuously. His faith became an example for all who participated, and in the process helped restore the faith of a nation in the God they loved but had lost sight of in their days of exile. For the change to become a lasting change, Nehemiah knew there was one more thing to be done. His mission wasn't just about rebuilding the walls of the city, it was also about rebuilding the people themselves, reestablishing their strong faith and trust in God. The people had to understand God's Word and confess their own sins so they could be fully restored. Nehemiah called everyone together and asked Ezra the priest to read the Holy Scriptures, "making it clear and giving the meaning so that the people could understand what was being read" (Nehemiah 8:8). There was much weeping as they listened and confessed their sins and the sins of their fathers.

Then one final instruction from Nehemiah: "'Go and enjoy choice food and sweet drinks, and send some to those who have nothing prepared. This day is sacred to our Lord. Do not grieve, for the joy of the LORD is your strength'" (v. 10).

Nehemiah understood the meaning of commitment and the importance of prayer when following God's call. He also understood that one person alone could not sustain the work for the long haul. A good leader takes others with him on the journey where ownership becomes broader and more self-sustaining. He cast a vision for others who would join in the task and success became the joy of all involved.

## International WMU Partners

One of the great unexpected joys of leading WMU has been the sisterhood with women in other countries. Our history is a story of shared leadership and purpose as together we seek to tell the story of Jesus to those who have never heard. When missionaries went out from the United States, the females, many with backgrounds like mine, looked for ways to equip other women in missions. They took with them the only framework they knew that worked—WMU. And so in many countries around the world WMU is strong. We share a common purpose, adapted to meet the culture of their people; but at its core, the same calling.

The more I realize all my counterparts do with much fewer resources, the more humbled I feel about all we have at our disposal. As a leader I am to be a good steward of our resources, frugal with spending, and preserving what I can of reserves for a sustainable future; but I think they know something we are just beginning to learn. It is not the available resources that determine our success, it is God's call; and when we are faithful to His call, He will provide just what is needed at the moment we need it. Their dependence on God for everything is a lesson we need to learn in our personal lives as well as our ministry.

WMU was first born outside the US in Brazil in 1908. While I have not visited their offices personally, it was a joy to send greetings to them for their 100th anniversary meeting and to receive some of their women in our offices in recent years. The next WMU was formed in Cuba in 1913, Nigeria and Mexico in 1919, and Japan in 1920. On the story goes of women in other lands catching a vision of what WMU organizers in 1888 saw as our responsibility to share the gospel, teach missions concepts, and develop models for ministry which would encourage and equip others to serve in Jesus' name. Having seen the work of some of these women leading in their national WMU ministries, I realize God is working in amazing ways to keep His story alive through men and women who serve in WMU today. Their stories of commitment are an inspiration for each of us who shares a love for God's mission.

# WMU in the Philippines

*It was nearing midnight when I arrived in Manila. What I thought might be a somewhat empty airport at that hour was far from it. People were pressing to get through customs, claiming their belongings packed in boxes, taped-up bags, or whatever they could manage when they left their previous destination. Once I found my suitcase and passed through customs and security, I was hit with the sultry heat of a summer night in the tropics. Throngs of people were trying to connect with drivers at the bustling airport. If there was an order to the lines for cars, no one seemed to care. With horns honking and people calling out to offer a ride, the night was filled with sound. Imagine my relief in the midst of the noise to hear the voice of Linda Dillworth, an American from Georgia, a fellow Baptist nurse and 30-plus-year veteran missionary to the Philippines. Linda and I had met a number of years ago, but it had been some time since we had seen each other. She guided me through the sea of faces to her car and we began the journey to the missionary guesthouse.*

*At midnight the streets of Manila were still full of people and vehicles were everywhere, especially the colorful jeepneys. After World War II leftover Jeeps were converted into public transportation with personalized names and glittering decorations covering the flatbed seats where 20 or more would crowd on for a ride. It was an amusing sight to see them careening across the lanes of traffic with people holding on for dear life. I had a sudden flash of the makeshift buses we had in the Caribbean where I had lived more than 30 years ago. Somehow the jeepneys seemed a lot sturdier and certainly much more fun in appearance. Arriving at the mission compound where numerous missionaries lived and worked, the guard motioned us into the fenced-in grounds and I finally began to relax. Linda was a gracious hostess who had thought of everything, including breakfast food and coffee so I could have a late morning the next day. I was grateful for her warm hospitality in a new place and settled in for much-needed rest.*

The following days were filled with meeting new people, learning about the country and the work of missionaries serving all across this chain of more than 7,000 islands. Manila is a city of contrasts. I was amazed, for instance, to see the extremely modern shopping mall with familiar stores, even a Krispy Kreme doughnut shop in the center and not far away a long row of makeshift houses with tin roofs. Driving around the city, I saw very high-end shops and high-rise apartment complexes; just a few feet away were shacks made from whatever a person could find selling their goods. Linda commented that the Philippines had its share of the very rich and the very poor with little middle class in between. What I observed that first day certainly seemed to support this thought.

Sunday morning arrived with new opportunities to meet the Filipino people. Driving to a church located in an impoverished section of the city, we saw the faces of hungry, homeless children everywhere. Some were begging, some washing windshields for a donation, and others just wandering aimlessly around the streets. My first impulse was to draw them all into my arms and give them the food and care they needed. But that was impossible at this moment in time. At the church we were greeted with open arms and hugs in abundance. The welcoming spirit of fellow Christians was genuine, something I have experienced in many other places around the world. With enthusiastic music and worship, lunch prepared by many of the women and shared by all, an afternoon of experiencing their native customs, including dance, began. Graceful dancers and unusual musical instruments filled the stage. While I knew it was coming, I was still not prepared for my turn at trying to maneuver between the bamboo poles in their most popular native dance, tinikling. Somewhere in the Philippines there is a movie of that less-than-graceful attempt, one I hope will never surface in the US.

In the midst of all the activity that day I became acquainted with Laura Raymundo, national WMU president for the Philippines, a beautiful woman with many gifts. She has an amazing voice, speaks with confidence, and yes, she can do tinikling without having her feet bruised by the poles. She and her husband, pastor of Paco Baptist Church, have a great vision for leading their church to minister among the poor in their community. Many of the children I observed near the church that morning were recipients of hot meals all throughout the week at the church because of this couple. She carries that same passion for ministry into her role as WMU president.

The Philippines is a massive land, making leadership a challenge. The country is divided into three key regions: Luzon, Visayas, and Mindanao. Following that same pattern of division, Laura leads a team of three regional presidents, all volunteers. Each region is broken down into manageable areas where volunteers work with local churches that share a common missions purpose. One day we gathered at the mission compound with representatives from several of the regions. I was humbled as I listened to their stories of personal sacrifice, to the struggles of rural missions work, the hardships of ministry in the megacities, and the challenges of distance between the islands. Travel was far from easy and finances were always a concern. Each voiced their desire to meet the needs of their people with a commitment to sharing the story of Jesus wherever they could. They press on because they know time is of the essence with the growing influence of Muslim extremists.

As they shared, I wondered how many of us would walk up and down the mountainous terrain of Mindanao or, in contrast, fight the massive traffic jams of Manila to engage people in missions learning and service as they do. We share the same purposes within our respective WMU organizations with a common heritage of missions at our core. Yet with all our resources, both in personnel and finances, one thing stood out: their passionate belief that WMU is the framework for propelling the Great Commission forward in the Philippines. When their convention was not able to grasp the urgency, for instance, for sending missionaries, the women organized, raised the funds, and began appointing women to go to the most critical places. When they saw the poverty in the communities around *where they lived, they organized their churches and began to feed and care for the hungry. It prompted me to question if our passion and commitment here in the US was anywhere near what I saw among this group of Baptist women in the Philippines. Their work was inspiring to say the least. I left the country a few days later with a fresh understanding of sacrifice and a renewed commitment to lead and serve others with the same joy I had seen among the women of this land.*

*Several weeks later, I turned on the news and, to my horror, saw the aftermath of a typhoon that hit the country. At one point it was reported that 80 percent of Manila was flooded, leaving thousands of families homeless. I found myself searching the TV screen for familiar faces and areas of town where I had just been. So much loss and damage among people who already had so little seemed overwhelming. I was relieved when word came that our WMU leaders and missionary families were safe. I was not surprised to learn that in the midst of their own difficulties, they were banding together to implement relief efforts providing food and shelter to those who needed assistance. While I could not go to assist them personally, I knew how and where to tap into financial resources that could help. The journey of partnership and sisterhood continues.*

## WMU in Korea

*That same spirit of missions commitment is found in Korea. In a previous book,* Live the Call, *I introduced my friend, Sook Jae Lee, executive director of Korea WMU. Sook Jae and I have continued to enjoy a long-distance friendship with the occasional opportunity to be together at meetings or when one of us visits the other's country. In 2009, it was my turn to visit Korea. I had the privilege of spending a week with her on what was my second trip to Seoul. It was a week filled with many different experiences as I became better acquainted with her beautiful country. From speaking at their national WMU event, to sharing leadership training with her officers, I was blessed by the warmth and genuine hospitality of the beautiful Korean women.*

*One day as I entered Sook Jae's office at the WMU building, I noticed a picture of retired missionary Lucy Wagner on the wall above her desk. She lovingly looked at that picture and said, "This is my American WMU mother!"*

*Her mother indeed and the esteemed mother of so many Korean WMU leaders today. It was Lucy Wagner, a young woman from Garden City, Missouri, who went to Korea in 1955 and helped nurture a brand-new ministry among Korean women—today that ministry is WMU. A self-supporting missions organization modeled after our own American WMU, we share a similar structure, logo, and purpose. Like many others in her day, Lucy Wagner answered God's call to missions and found a major part of her job was to equip the Korean people to become Great Commission people in their own right. She implemented the one tool she knew best—WMU.*

*Lucy's entire life is a testimony of what God can do despite the hindrances of everyday life that might keep us from answering His call. When Lucy was 11 years old, her mom died suddenly. That next year she found faith in Jesus Christ and began a journey of learning what it meant to follow Jesus. When she was in high school, another tragedy; she lost her father. Thanks to an aunt and uncle who stepped in and continued to nurture and care for her, Lucy continued to grow as a Christian. In college, she was a member of YWA (Young Woman's Auxiliary), the forerunner to today's collegiate missions organizations. While serving as president of that organization, she made a public commitment to missions during a youth revival in 1948. Not long after making that commitment, she became friends with a young Korean girl who one day looked at her with tears in her eyes and said, "Maybe you come to my country!"*

God has a plan for each of our lives. He had a plan for Lucy despite the grief and loss of her parents early in her life, despite the challenges of travel during post–World War II years. She served in a place where being a single woman living in a very family-oriented culture was difficult. And yet the Lord led Lucy to look beyond all those things that would prevent her from going. Because she went, because she was faithful in overcoming the difficulties that could have prevented her service, the lives of untold numbers were changed as they learned about the love of Jesus.

Like Lucy, Sook Jae was living out her call to missions serving as a missionary nurse but was soon tapped for leadership by those who came into WMU leadership after Lucy. She traveled alone to the US to attend seminary and learn how to lead. Alabama WMU provided an internship at one point so she could have firsthand experience working in a ministry setting. Today she leads this impressive organization in developing missions organizations for the churches, building a home for retired pastors in Korea, and helping Korean women living in China start missions organizations in their churches, all in hopes they, too, will catch a vision for missions.

Today the early efforts of Lucy Wagner and those who followed after her, including Sook Jae, have resulted in a vision for sending missionaries of their own. Approximately 500 Korean missionaries serve in more than 45 countries around the world. With the missions vision of Sook Jae and others, they have a strong prayer and financial support system for their missionaries, a partnership that makes it possible for individuals to hear and answer God's call wherever He leads them.

## WMU in Africa

In Africa, many of the nations have varying degrees of a WMU organization. While I have not traveled to Africa, our current national president, Debby Akerman, went in 2011 to meet with representatives from six nations who wanted to learn the new ways of WMU work. They spent several days together discussing how to lead women to pray, give, and serve in missions themselves. They learned how to organize girls into missions groups (Girls in Action®) so they can learn about missions at a young age. The structures are all different with Nigeria being the most established, publishing its own curriculum, to Burkina Faso, the youngest, having organized most recently. There have been starts and stops for some due to war, famine, and natural disasters changing the face of their nation; but the commitment to missions and telling the story of Jesus never left their hearts.

In Liberia, Baptist work was established long ago. Churches were built, schools were started, and then war came. Over and over people fought for a variety of reasons. Many lives were lost and a nation was destroyed.

After years of war, a tentative peace accord came and the country began to rebuild. By this time Baptist missionaries were no longer living in the country. Many former pastors and leaders were either out of the country or had died in the war. How would they begin to rebuild their churches and the Baptist schools that had once been so strong? The people could have decided it was too hard to start over. They could have said, "Why should we try?" But that was not their answer. Individuals stepped up; and in the midst of intermittent strife, Baptist work resumed.

Today schools are being rebuilt through the leadership of young men like Olu Menjay and Eddie Gibson, boys who grew up through Royal Ambassadors® (RA®) camps, the boy's missions organizations, and the teachings of the Liberian Baptist churches. Young men, who fled the war and came to America for an education, have returned with a vision for the future among Baptist work and their nation as a whole. I've had the privilege of connecting with both of these men through the years, sometimes here in the United States but also in places where we were both attending meetings to dialogue about how to best overcome the challenges we each face. Both are investing themselves in the future by helping the youth of Liberia receive a quality education and gain an understanding that God has a plan for their lives, and it is not constant war.

WMU has always found creative ways to partner with our international friends. Much of the residential school that was once a part of the Baptist missionary compound in Liberia, for instance, was destroyed, including access to clean water. Through a grant from our Pure Water, Pure Love fund, a water system has been restored. We've communicated the need for volunteers and many have helped with rebuilding the school and renovating the damaged houses on the property. Educators from the US have made multiple trips to train their teachers and provide resources to help children, especially girls, have the funds to attend school again. There is hope, but it requires commitment on the part of leaders like Olu Menjay and others who believe in Liberia's future.

What had once been a strong WMU organization in Liberia, teaching missions and having GA and RA children's camps, had also all but disappeared during the years of war. The children's camp where many special camping events had once taken place was also decimated. Today, Olivia Williams is providing leadership as she serves as their WMU president. Olivia and I have not met personally, but the wonderful thing about the Internet is we can communicate frequently and work together as we identify ways our staff can help them in their rebuilding efforts. She knows the importance of developing new leadership and is gathering a core of younger women, teaching them to lead and prepare for the future of their churches in the area of missions. With very meager resources, she and others have restarted GA and RA groups in the churches, rebuilt the camp, and restarted their summer program where girls can come away from the difficulties of life at home and learn about Jesus, His Word, and missions. You see, implanted in the hearts of the Liberian believers from their early beginnings as a free nation was an understanding that each of us, regardless of our circumstances, is to embrace the whole world, to love all peoples, and to see that every person has a chance to hear the *gospel. Olivia, Olu, Eddie, and others are committed to keeping the story of Jesus alive, planting it in the hearts of its future generation because they have experienced His power to change their lives. They know He wants to do the same for the Liberian people.*

Nehemiah models the importance of personal responsibility for our faith and following God's call while at the same time accepting a responsibility for taking others with us on the journey. The heart of WMU from the very beginning has been that the nations of the world might come to faith in Christ. That desire is paired with a commitment to demonstrate faith through acts of love and service after the manner of Jesus. We accepted the responsibility long ago to equip women and girls in particular as well as all of the members of the church in understanding and finding their place of radical involvement in the mission of God. But it begins with one person hearing God's call to love the world and inspiring those around them to do the same.

Our reach around the world today began when a person committed to missions and appreciative of the framework of WMU to help engage others in missions shared the story. It grew from the missionary who trained one woman to a legion of committed followers of Christ training one more. Our strength, and the future of any organization or church, lies in the commitment of one woman, one man, one boy, and one girl to open their hearts to the voice of God and allow Him to guide them.

# Reflections

With a commitment to prayer and knowing God's Word, the foundation is set for the journey to begin. It is a lifelong journey of commitment to follow Christ each day.

# Conclusion: The Next Chapter

*C*ountless stories are yet to be told about individuals who have followed Jesus down a path of sacrifice and service. Their stories are too numerous to tell within the pages of this book; rather, they reside in the hearts and minds of all who know them or have been touched by their kindness. Our story began with Peter and John, two ordinary, common men who demonstrated their humanness in many ways while they followed Jesus. But after the Resurrection, after they saw the risen Jesus, after the Holy Spirit had filled their lives with power, they became more than common men. They were men with an uncommon calling; and in the face of much persecution, they could not stop telling what they had seen and heard.

After Peter and John healed the beggar at the Temple gate (Acts 4), faced the Sanhedrin, and spent a night in jail, their troubles were not over. It was actually just the beginning of a journey with many challenges that would cost them dearly. In the very next chapter we read where they were brought back before the same group after their confrontation with Ananias and Sapphira. They had continued to preach and had "performed many miraculous signs and wonders among the people" (Acts 5:12). Their actions angered the religious leaders even more, so they arrested Peter and John again. They reminded them about their previous instructions to cease teaching; and once again Peter responded boldly, "We must obey God rather than men!" (v. 29).

In the midst of trying to determine what to do with them, Gamaliel, a teacher of the Law, stepped in and advised the

Sanhedrin to release them. His words were very telling to those who were present and for us today.

*"Let them go! For if their purpose or activity is of human origin, it will fail. But if it is from God, you will not be able to stop these men; you will only find yourselves fighting against God" (Acts 5:38–39).*

When our calling is of God, nothing can stop us. When we come to Him in faith, experience the wonder of His grace and forgiveness, the greatest joy comes from finding ways we can give back through service to others. Author Os Guinness in his book *The Call: Finding and Fulfilling the Central Purpose of Your Life* reminds us, "The motive, the initiative, and the action of calling are entirely God's and all of grace. Christ does not choose us because we are worth choosing, but simply because in his grace he loves us and chooses us—he calls us, in fact, despite all that he had to do to seal that choice in blood."

Peter and John had experienced the power of Jesus to turn their lives from one of routine to one of eternal significance. Because of the radical nature of the gospel to impact others in the same way, they could do no less than what they were doing. Think about the Peter we read about in Luke 22, for instance, who boasted he would never stumble after Jesus tried to help the disciples understand the meaning of greatness. And yet, it was Peter who followed Jesus into the courtyard on the night He was arrested and not only did he stumble, multiple times he denied he even knew Jesus. Peter, the decisive, quick-acting disciple who cut off the ear of a soldier with his sword only to hear the rebuke of Jesus and witness Him heal that same ear. Peter, who had experienced so much shame and remorse after the Crucifixion, received even more grace and forgiveness after the Resurrection. So deep was his experience with Jesus he could not possibly keep it to himself.

Philip Yancey wrote in *What's So Amazing About Grace?*, "*Grace means there is nothing we can do to make God love us more*—no amount of spiritual calisthenics and renunciations, no amount of knowledge gained from seminaries and divinity schools, no amount of crusading on behalf of righteous causes. *And grace means there is nothing we can do to make God love us less.*"

Paul described this profound kind of love in Romans 8:35, 37.

*Who shall separate us from the love of Christ? Shall trouble or hardship or persecution or famine or nakedness or danger or sword? . . . No, in all these things we are more than conquerors through him who loved us.*

After listing all the things that cannot separate us, he ends this passage with the assurance that nothing can separate us from the love of God because of what Jesus has done for us. Peter and John knew this by personal experience and they simply wanted everyone else to know it as well.

As an ordinary person, a common man or woman, have you received an uncommon calling? Have you experienced grace in such a way that you know there is nothing you can do to make God love you more and, likewise, there is nothing you can do to make God love you less? When that kind of love and grace is a part of our experience, there is nothing we can go through in life that will rob us of our joy. Our story of overcoming becomes a vehicle for helping others discover their own story and how God wants to use them in His service.

The Book of Acts continues to trace the miracles performed and the boldness with which Peter and John professed their faith.

The critical issue of the Christian faith being for all people beyond the Jews, specifically the Gentiles being acceptable in God's sight, was settled because Peter allowed God to change his own perspective and others followed. Because of Peter, John, and the other apostles, the church grew and you and I have the opportunity to know Jesus in a personal way today.

Scripture is silent about the death of Peter, but historical accounts indicate he died most likely in Rome. Traditions say he watched his wife crucified first; and after requesting to be hung upside down because he was unworthy of the same kind of death as Jesus, he was crucified in the same place. All of the apostles but John became martyrs, as Jesus had warned in the closing verses of the Gospel of John.

As the last of the apostles to die, John lived into old age but exiled on the island of Patmos much of that time. In his own way he must have suffered from such crude living conditions and isolation. Despite all the persecution and personal suffering, he influenced the churches and all of Christianity with his prophetic words in Revelation. Next to Luke and Paul, John wrote more of the New Testament than any other writer.

But their death was not the end of their influence. Their faithfulness to Christ and His teachings, their boldness in sharing what they had seen and heard impacted their world and all future generations for the sake of the gospel. Peter reminds us we, too, have a story to tell, a responsibility to carry on for the future. "To this you were called, because Christ suffered for you, leaving you an example that you should follow in his steps" (1 Peter 2:21).

My story began at home. Early in life Jesus became the focal point of my life story. As I experienced the loss of family, the calling to missions as a nurse, and then as the leader of an organization that supports the missions calling of others, Jesus has carried me through, giving grace and wisdom each step of the way.

I am convinced that the love of God is deeper and wider than my mind can ever imagine. For reasons I may never know, He loves me despite all my failures and celebrates with me all my successes with great joy. I have become a part of the greatest story ever told. For that reason I join Peter and John in declaring, "Judge for yourselves whether it is right in God's sight to obey you rather than God. For we cannot help speaking about what we have seen and heard." And because of Him, the story lives on . . .

# Bibliography

**Chapter 1**
Brainy Quote. "George Eliot Quotes." http://brainyquote.com/quotes/authors/g/george_eliot_3.html (accessed September 11, 2011).

Yancey, Philip. *What's So Amazing About Grace?* Grand Rapids, MI: Zondervan Publishing House, 1997.

**Chapter 2**
PuebloDirect.com. "Storytellers and Figurines." http://www.pueblodirect.com/storytellers2.html (accessed February 28, 2012).

Baylor University. The Baylor Alumni Network. http://www.baylor.edu/network/index.php?id=65953 (accessed August 12, 2011).

Johnston, Sammie. *The Dream Builders: The Story of the Forts of Africa.* Birmingham, AL: New Hope Publishers, 1989.

Wikipedia. "Jim Elliot." http://en.wikipedia.org/wiki/Jim_Elliot (accessed February 29, 2012).

At Any Cost. "Did They Have to Die." http://www.atanycost.org/DidTheyHaveToDie.htm (accessed February 29, 2012).

———. "Story." http://www.atanycost.org/discuss.htm (accessed February 29, 2012).

Saint, Steve. "Did They Have to Die?" *Christianity Today* 40, no. 10 (1996): 20. http://www.christianitytoday.com/global/pf.cgi?/ct/6ta/6ta020.html (accessed February 29, 2012).

Baptist Press. "Martha Myers Sculpture Dedicated." May 18. 2007. http://www.bpnews.net/bpnews.asp?ID=25688 (accessed November 14, 2011).

**Chapter 3**
Drawing to the Rock. "Kerry and Twyla Jackson." http://www.drawingtotherock.com/msc/ (accessed November 21, 2011).

Royal, Claudia. *Storytelling.* Nashville: Broadman Press, 1955.

Hastings, Robert J. *Tinyburg Tales.* Nashville: Broadman Press, 1983.

Hastings, Robert J. *Tinyburg Revisited.* Nashville: Broadman Press, 1988.

Tinyburg Tales. "Tinyburg Tales Broadcasts." http://www.tinyburgtales.com/ (accessed February 28, 2012).

http://robertjhastings.com/ (accessed February 28, 2012).

Arab Woman Today Ministries. "About AWT/Vision & Objectives." http://www
.awtministries.com/english/vision.php (accessed October 4, 2011).
Arab Woman Today Ministries. "About AWT." http://www.awtministries.com/english/
aboutawt.php (accessed October 4, 2011).

Coventry Cathedral. "Our Ministry of Reconciliation." http://www.coventrycathedral.
org.uk/about-us/our-reconciliation-ministry.php (accessed February 28, 2012).

———. "Our History." http://www.coventrycathedral.org.uk/about-us/our-history.php
(accessed February 28, 2012).

Wikipedia. "Josefina de Vasconcellos." http://en.wikipedia.org/wiki/Josefina_de
_Vasconcellos (accessed February 28, 2012).

Nouwen, Henri J. M. *The Return of the Prodigal Son.* New York: Doubleday/Image, 1994.
Quoted in Yancey, Philip. *What's So Amazing About Grace?* Grand Rapids, MI: Zondervan
Publishing House, 1997.

### Chapter 4
Field, Taylor. *A Church Called Graffiti: Finding Grace on the Lower East Side.* Nashville:
Broadman & Holman Publishers, 2001.

Lee, Wanda. "From Missionary Ridge." *Missions Mosaic,* October 2011.

The Water Page. "Current Status." http://africanwater.org/basic_needs.htm (accessed
February 28. 2012).

2005 WMU Annual Report. Birmingham, AL: Woman's Missionary Union, SBC.

### Chapter 5
Barstow, Sammie Jo. "Chasing Hope—Keeping Hope." *Missions Mosaic,* January 2011.

Rezahi, Jamal. *Chasing Hope.* Maitland, FL: Xulon Press, 2006.

### Chapter 6
Fowler, Franklin T. "The History of Southern Baptist Medical Missions." *Baptist History
and Heritage* 10 (October 1975): 194–203.

Ellison, Nina. *Mama John.* Birmingham, AL: New Hope Publishers, 1996.

Staines, Terri. "For the Love of Christ: Ministering to the Needs of the Poor." *Missions
Mosaic,* November 2011.

Cross-Purposes. "Stacy Smith–November 2006." http://www.cross-purpose.org/stacy
_smith.htm (accessed February 28, 2012).

Whitfield, Amy. "Mullins Awarded WMU's Top Honor." WMU press release, June 12,
2006.

Haven of Rest Family Ministries. "How We Came About." http://www.freewebs.com/havenofrest/aboutus.htm (accessed August 12, 2011).

**Chapter 7**
Louisiana State Penitentiary. http://www.doc.louisiana.gov/LSP/ (accessed February 28, 2012).

Foster, Mary. "Angola Prison in La. Offers Ministry Degree to Inmates." Associated Press. January 6, 2010. http://www.correctionsone.com/pc_print.asp?vid=1986507 (accessed September 22, 2011).

**Chapter 8**
"Restoring Lives Through CWJC." *Missions Mosaic,* June 2011.

Richardson, Amy W. "Texas Teacher Receives GA Distinction Award." WMU press release, June 11, 2007.

Walters, Julie. "Clayton Recognized as GA of Distinction." WMU press release, June 16, 2004.

————. "Cranford Receives Dr. Martha Myers GA Alumna of Distinction Award." WMU press release, June 14, 2010.

Gable, Jessie. "Arkansas Missions Leader Receives Dellanna O'Brien Leadership Award." WMU press release, June 22, 2009.

MacArthur, John. *Twelve Ordinary Men.* Nashville: W Publishing Group, 2002.

**Chapter 9**
Hunt, Rosalie. *The Story of WMU.* Birmingham, AL: Woman's Missionary Union, 2006.

Hansen, Collin. "Christian History Corner: Liberia's Troubled Past—and Present." *Christianity Today,* July 1, 2003. http://www.christianitytoday.com/ct/article_print.html?is=10670 (accessed August 30, 2011).

International Mission Board. "Liberia Seminary Reopens after 7 Years of Civil War." IMB press release, March 23, 1999. http://www.imb.org/main/news/details.asp?LanguageID=1709&StoryID=319 (accessed August 30, 2011).

**Conclusion**
Guinness, Os. *The Call: Finding and Fulfilling the Central Purpose of Your Life.* Nashville: W Publishing Group, 1998. Quoted in Lee, Wanda. *Live the Call.* Birmingham, AL: New Hope Publishers, 2006.

Yancey, Philip. *What's So Amazing About Grace?* Grand Rapids, MI: Zondervan Publishing House, 1997.

Barclay, William. *The Master's Men.* Nashville: Abingdon Press, 1959.

# Additional Resources on Missional Living

**Beyond Me**
*Living a You-First Life in a Me-First World*
Kathi Macias
ISBN-13: 978-1-59669-220-6
N084143 • $12.99

**Faces in the Crowd**
*Reaching Your International
Neighbor for Christ*
Donna S. Thomas
ISBN-13: 978-1-59669-205-3
N084131 • $12.99

**Live Sent**
*You Are a Letter*
Jason C. Dukes
ISBN-13: 978-1-59669-315-9
N114149 • $14.99

NEW HOPE
PUBLISHERS

Available in bookstores everywhere. For information about these books or any
New Hope product, visit newhopedigital.com.

New Hope® Publishers is a division of WMU®, an international organization that challenges Christian believers to understand and be radically involved in God's mission.
For more information about WMU, go to: wmu.com.
More information about New Hope books can be found at newhopedigital.com.
New Hope books may be purchased at your local bookstore.

Use the QR reader on your
smartphone to visit us online at
newhopedigital.com

If you've been blessed by this book, we would like to hear your story.
The publisher and author welcome your comments and
suggestions at: newhopereader@wmu.org.